BRIDGING THE GAP

Previous titles by Lesley Roessing

The Right to Read: Response Journals That Increase Comprehension
No More "Us" and "Them": Classroom Lessons and Activities to Promote Peer Respect
Comma Quest: The Rules They Followed—The Sentences They Saved

BRIDGING THE GAP

Reading Critically
and
Writing Meaningfully
to Get to the Core

Lesley Roessing

ROWMAN & LITTLEFIELD
Lanham • Boulder • New York • London

Published by Rowman & Littlefield
A wholly owned subsidiary of The Rowman & Littlefield Publishing Group, Inc.
4501 Forbes Boulevard, Suite 200, Lanham, Maryland 20706
www.rowman.com

16 Carlisle Street, London W1D 3BT, United Kingdom

British Library Cataloguing in Publication Information Available

ISBN 978-1-4758-1091-2 (cloth : alk. paper) — ISBN 978-1-4758-1092-9 (pbk. : alk. paper) — ISBN 978-1-4758-1093-6 (electronic)

∞™ The paper used in this publication meets the minimum requirements of
American National Standard for Information Sciences—Permanence of Paper
for Printed Library Materials, ANSI/NISO Z39.48-1992.

Printed in the United States of America

To my Ridley students who shared their stories and led me to find mine.

To my family and friends who helped to build those stories.

And to those teachers who are willing to help students write and read their stories to begin "bridging the gap(s)."

CONTENTS

FOREWORD
The Real Thing

Anyone who has begun to think, places some portion of the world in jeopardy.

—John Dewey

I was in my car listening to Spotify, the streaming music service with over twenty million songs. At a stoplight I had typed in "Beatles" and waited for the music to start as I sped up the road. It started with an oldie, "I Want to Hold Your Hand," the song I first heard when I was in third grade. "Oh, yeah, I'll tell you something I think you'll understand. When I say that something, I want to hold your hand . . ."

For a second or two, I had a sweet memory of my two friends, Mark Veillux and John Kenney, and I singing the song in front of the class to start the morning in third grade. I was Paul, Mark was John, and John was George. Ringo was the imaginary guy behind us that we would nod to occasionally. We closed our eyes and shook our heads on the "I want to hold your haaaaaaannnd" line to get the full Beatle excitement. I'm not sure the girls were that impressed, but for just a brief moment, we were the Beatles. And our teacher, in a moment of spontaneous wisdom, had granted it be so.

As I listened now, driving down the interstate, something was terribly wrong. The chords were the same, the arrangements the same, and the voices the same, but something indescribable was missing. I glanced at my smartphone and instantly saw the problem. This was not the Beatles. This was a Beatles tribute band, a group of four men whose sole purpose is to replicate Beatles music note for note, word for word to adoring Beatles fans. They were a live band pretending to be a dead band. They were a group with a past, but no present, and no future, a Xerox machine with instruments.

I started to meditate on what was missing in a tribute band's performing a Beatles song, compared to a real artist like Stevie Wonder covering "We Can Work It Out" on his *Signed, Sealed & Delivered* album. Wonder interpreted the song; he brought his unique spirit and voice to the Beatles' words. The Beatles tribute band was not allowed to interpret or reimagine the song. Their performance was measured on how well they could imitate and duplicate the Beatles standard performance.

In a flash, I had an uncomfortable realization about what is really wrong with our mandated Common Core State Standards approach to education and the standards-based assessments that are inextricably linked to it. We are turning our students, teachers, and administrators into tribute bands whose goal is to replicate past outcomes of learning to meet basic measurable test requirements. Creativity, passion, and interpretation, along with the magical yearning you hear in the real John Lennon's wail or the sweet, creamy calm of Paul McCartney's croon, have been put aside in favor of the timid, carefully measured, Velveeta versions that never break a sweat.

Lesley Roessing's practical book *Bridging the Gap* helps to reverse this disturbing standardization trend in American education by helping students find their own stories. Its approach to memoir writing aims to engage students in a passionate inquiry into the essential questions: Who are you? Where are you from? Where are you going? These are questions that lead to personal transformation, passionate engagement, and remarkable writing that inspires students to find their true voices in other genres.

Using mentor texts as diverse as Marcel Proust, Billy Collins, George Ella Lyon, and a host of others, Roessing takes students and teachers on a journey of self-discovery, and along the way teaches core literacy skills of poetry, literary analysis, and narrative and informational writing. Chapters of this highly practical book help students to find moments and events to write about, read published memoirs with a writer's eye, find stories and odes in objects, and interpret places and events. In short, the lessons in this book break down memoir into focused, manageable lessons that any teacher can use to build a life-changing unit on memoir writing.

When students start to write their stories, when they start to value their experience, something happens that cannot be measured by any test or quantitative assessment. It is a look in the eye, a nod, a confident swagger that starts to appear in all the writing they do. Call it style, call it voice, call it "writing sentences of varying lengths"; I call it passion, and that is the one thing that will create a lifelong writer.

—Barry Lane, author of *After "The End": Teaching and Learning Creative Revision; The Reviser's Toolbox; 51 Wacky We-Search Reports: Face the Facts with Fun; Why We Must Run With Scissors: Voice Lesson in Persuasive Writing; But How Do You Teach Writing: A Simple Guide for All Teachers*

ACKNOWLEDGMENTS

I have wanted to write this book and share the power of memoir writing with teachers for many years. I witnessed this positive force year after year with my students at Ridley Middle School, Ridley Park, Pennsylvania, and my wish is that students everywhere have the chance to read critically and write meaningfully about what matters and what is accessible—to them. I thank my former students for their willingness to engage in my lessons, participate in all our activities ("An eighth-grade Show 'n Tell? Seriously?") and, most of all, share their lives, their hearts, and their writings. I do think that the unit described in this book led each and every one to their best writings of the year, and I appreciate the chance to share those writings as "Student Samples" with other educators and their students through this book.

Grateful Acknowledgements to . . .

Sara Jane Doubleday and her principal, Allison Schuster-Jones, of Godley Station School in Pooler, Georgia, and Donna Martin and her principal, Denise Smith, of Robert Smalls Middle School in Beaufort, South Carolina, for inviting me into their classrooms to work and write with their students who also have shared their conversations and stories;

Patricia Wachholz, dean of Armstrong State University's College of Education, who for five years has supported my writing and working with teachers and students in the Savannah and Georgia Coastal school districts;

The fellows—and my friends—of the Coastal Savannah Writing Project, excellent teachers who were willing to learn and try new ways to write and read with their students and pushed me to further develop and refine my thoughts about reading and writing;

Julie Warner, my technology advisor, who contributed the digital literacy suggestions in Chapter 11, and Carol Raymond, supportive friend and first reader-editor of my draft manuscript;

Barry Lane, author and friend, who encouraged me to write this book and wrote the entertaining and memoir-filled Foreword for the book;

My family—Chuck, Meg, Matt, and Julia—who listened to me endlessly talk and obsess about yet another project and, along with my parents and sister, helped me to create my memories;

Editor Tom Koerner for agreeing to publish another book for me; Carlie Wall for all her assistance and suggestions (and quick replies); and everyone at Rowman & Littlefield who turned the manuscript into a book; and

ACKNOWLEDGMENTS

I am grateful to the authors and publishers who generously permitted us to reprint their writings, used as mentor texts in this manuscript:

"I Am From" by Doug Gavetti. Originally printed in *No More "Us" and "Them": Classroom Activities & Lessons to Promote Peer Respect* by Lesley Roessing (R&L Education), ©2012. Reprinted by permission of Rowman & Littlefield Education.

"Where I Am From" by Janel Moore. Originally printed in *No More "Us" and "Them": Classroom Activities & Lessons to Promote Peer Respect* by Lesley Roessing (R&L Education), ©2012. Reprinted by permission of Rowman & Littlefield Education.

"On Turning Ten" from *The Art of Drowning* by Billy Collins, ©1995. Reprinted by permission of the University of Pittsburgh Press.

"What I Remember About Sixth Grade" from *Late Night Calls* by Mark Vinz (New Rivers Press), ©1992. Reprinted by permission of the author.

"When Lobsters Run Free," from the *Philadelphia Inquirer*, by David Holahan, ©April 23, 2006. Reprinted by permission of the author.

"Where I'm From" from *Where I'm From, Where Poems Come From* by George Ella Lyon (Absey & Company, Inc.), ©1999. Reprinted by permission of the author.

"Ode to Pablo's Tennis Shoes" from *Neighborhood Odes* by Gary Soto. Copyright © 1992 by Gary Soto. Reprinted by permission of Houghton Mifflin Harcourt Publishing Company. All rights resrved.

And those teachers and students who generously permitted us to reprint their memoirs, presented as Teacher Models and Student Samples in this manuscript:

Mary Kate Reilly
Nicole Brestowski
Andrew Karahalis
Jennifer Levy
Kate Ament
Christine McDonald
Kyle Firth
Emily Primmer
Marissa Picardi
Janel Moore
Lacey Field
Paulina Tawil
Romeo Sepulveda
Kathy O'Donnell
Douglas Gavetti
P. J. Artese
Tyler Johnson
Chelsea Palo
Anthony Murgidi
Kevin Shirley

INTRODUCTION

The How, When, and Why of Memoir Writing

It's just after school, and all my current students have left.

"Hi, Mrs. Roessing." I look up. A former student enters my room, a second teenage girl in tow.

"I wanted to introduce you to Sam."

I smiled. I knew exactly to whom Mary Kate was referring. I had wanted to meet Sam for two years. I actually felt like I already knew her.

During her eighth-grade memoir unit, Mary Kate had written about Sam and their friendship in a free-verse poem that was, and still is, one of the best pieces of student writing I have read, a poem that had been selected by Poetry Alive! as its poem of the month.

> It is as cold as death
> Yet the air is
> tingling—full
> of youth and time.
> Time for us to while away
> never knowing the future is almost here.
> Parks
> Parks are for baseball players and schemers
> and Dreamers
> like me and Sam.
> Our cheeks are stung and flushed pink like watermelons from
> faraway summer.
> They clash with the black of the nine o' clock sky.
> Almost as black as coal but not quite.
> There's some blue.
> True blue for forever friends
> like me and Sam.
> Sliding, cheering, screaming
> down the once silent hill we glide
> coming to a jerking stop at the end.
> Like lather, rinse, repeat,
> we climb, sled, repeat
> until our noses are numb and our legs are cramped.
> We lay, softly,

and listen to the sounds of home.
The chain swing swaying, creaking.
The screen doors opening and closing.
The Blue Route humming on the bridge above.
We talked
on and on
about nothing and everything.
If you could go back and count the snowflakes lying on that
hallowed ground,
Add the Christmas lights on every tree in Swarthmore,
And multiply that by the small footprints we left,
you might get how many times we laughed.
And for the rest of my life
whenever I see the snow caressing the curve of the
nine o' clock sky,
I'll remember how fast that night went.
And hope this night lasts longer
for a couple of dreamers
like Sam and me.

                        —Mary Kate Reilly, 2006

The poem, written by an eighth grader, was skillfully comprised of a variety of effective writing techniques and was especially notable for its wealth of literary devices. Was it the choice of topic, as well as the strategies acquired to choose the most effective topic, that gave this young author something meaningful about which to write? Was it the numerous memoir mentor texts in divergent genres that the class read, deconstructed, and critically analyzed as examples of good writing and effective skills?

Was this young poet's skill a result of the teacher models by which I illustrated ways to craft text from memories using those same techniques that we analyzed and named? Was it due to the writing and revision lessons; the daily focus lessons on poetic devices, word choice, voice, sentence fluency, and organization? The impressiveness of the writing probably was due to all these experiences, plus natural talent on the part of the adolescent writer.

MEMOIR AS A BRIDGE ACROSS THE ACHIEVEMENT GAP

Research supports the fact that prior knowledge is a major determinant of academic achievement. Memoir is one area in which all students come to the lessons—reading and writing— with background knowledge.

Every child has a past filled with experiences and personal stories, and all adolescents have something of value to say and share. Memoir writing values these experiences and levels the playing field as all children—rich or poor, culturally diverse, academically "proficient" or "basic"—inherently have the essential "material" necessary to achieve memoir writing. In this way, memoir writing bridges the achievement gap. Students' pasts contain the topics about which to write meaningfully. Writers also can read critically when comparing an author's tales of childhood experiences to their own as memoir gives readers a purpose to read and valid connections to make.

Not all students have the prior knowledge, skill, or motivation to write to prompts on standardized tests, but once writers learn to write meaningfully on topics that matter, they can transfer those skills to other topics, even to "on-demand" writing tasks.

MEMOIR WRITING LEADS TO MORE MEANINGFUL WRITING

Teachers need to coach developing writers to discover and craft their personal stories. It is also our responsibility to impart the joy and power of writing. Children, especially adolescents and young adolescents, write more willingly and effectively about what interests them—themselves. Quality of writing improves when writers write about what they know, what they have experienced.

In that way, memoir writing, specifically, induces students to write more, write better, and write more willingly and meaningfully. When students are motivated to write, they want to write well and they want their writings to be effective. As Donald Murray Pulitzer-prize winning journalist, teacher, and author of books on writing, remarked, "You can command writing, but you can't command good writing." (Kahn, 2010, p. 16) Memoir writing elevates the topics on which the writing is based and, in so doing, elevates writing. Developing literacy skills in our adolescents, through the most appropriate means and the most effective strategies that engage them, will make them better communicators and consumers better prepared for college and career.

Teachers need to assist emerging writers in acquiring a variety of means and strategies to brainstorm and generate topics that are meaningful—giving them choices of *what* they write—and teach them a variety of tools and methods to express themselves successfully—providing options in *how* they write. A unit in writing should impart skills and strategies that writers can transfer to any writing for any purpose—narrative, informative, and opinion or argument writing—and audience.

MEMOIR AS A BRIDGE BETWEEN FICTION AND NONFICTION READING

Students view fiction and nonfiction text as completely different "species," and many teachers teach fiction and nonfiction reading and narrative and informative writing in completely different ways. The Common Core State Standards encourage teachers to introduce more nonfiction reading and informative writing; therefore, there needs to be a bridge between the two "worlds," especially as student reading comprehension and writing is declining as adolescents read and write more complex texts.

Memoir, which is narrative nonfiction, is that perfect bridge between the two modes. Students read information and facts about others through narrative structure as they write information and facts about themselves through narrative structure, meeting both Common Core State Standards in Literature and in Informational Texts and in Narrative Writing and in Informative/Explanatory Writing. Teaching memoir reading and writing can be based on, and meet, the majority of Common Core State Standards in reading, writing, speaking, and listening, as well as the language standards.

In Common Core English Language Arts Standard 10: Range, Quality, & Complexity—Range of Text Types for 6–12, "Students in grades 6–12 apply the Reading standards to the following range of text types, with texts selected from a broad range of cultures and periods"; "memoirs" are specifically listed under Informational Text: Literacy Nonfiction and Historical, Scientific, and Technical Texts.

MEMOIR TO MEET COMMON CORE STATE STANDARDS IN ARGUMENT WRITING

Memoir writing can also lead to more effective opinion and argument writing, meeting Common Core State Standards in Argument Writing. Through writing memoir, writers discover and uncover their own passions and convictions, leading them to choose more effective argument topics; readers are introduced to the roots of the passions and convictions of others as they read memoirs.

In addition, response to memoir reading, as delineated in the various lessons in this book, will help students meet additional Common Core argument requirements to "support claim(s) with logical reasoning and relevant evidence, using accurate, credible sources" as students learn to critique memoir readings in discussions and response journals.

MEMOIR AS A BRIDGE BETWEEN READING AND WRITING

Chapter 3 focuses on connecting reading and writing, and teaching students to read like a writer. The following chapters share reading and writing connection assignments. As students study a variety of memoir techniques and topics in class, writers can observe how published authors handle the same techniques and topics and, in that way, employ these readings as individual mentor texts. This practice teaches writers to read like writers, noticing and noting what they observe, and leads to increased comprehension as they are guided to respond in writing to what they read.

THE ARRANGEMENT OF THE BOOK

The memoir writing-reading unit throughout this book is designed so that writers

- learn and apply a variety of strategies to brainstorm and mine their memories for writeable moments;
- experience and analyze model memoirs in a variety of genres:
  - short-story and novel-length prose,
  - poetry in divergent forms: free-verse, rhyming, limericks, sonnets, . . .
  - songs and lyrics,
  - speeches and stand-up routines,
  - picture books,
  - plays,
  - essays,
  - news and magazine articles;
- practice drafting memoirs and synthesizing experiences about
  - ages or time periods in their lives,
  - possessions and mementos,
  - places,
  - people and relationships,
  - crises and defining moments and events,
  - their roots;
- evaluate and choose one, two, or three of their rough drafts (depending on grade-level and time constraints) to take to publication stage, through application of revision lessons that focus on the traits of writing:
  - discovering and uncovering ideas and developing those ideas,
  - organizing their writings in the most effective ways,
  - writing with style, voice, and sentence fluency,
  - editing for conventions;
- appreciate the distinctions of different genres so to purposefully publish in the genre most effective for their memoir;
- master writing techniques by means of mentor texts in diverse media and through teacher models and student examples;
- read memoirs, noting and reflecting on how and what the author writes, reading like writers;
- meet Common Core State Standards or state equivalents in reading, writing, speaking, and listening.

Bridging the Gap outlines a variety of successful methods for motivating and encouraging students, in particular reluctant writers and readers, to write and read more, thereby writing and comprehending better, and elevating the writing and reading of proficient writers and readers. The book also introduces and describes practices that may be unfamiliar or unclear to educators and the manner that these practices fit into a writing curriculum focused on any mode (type) or genre (format):

- read-alouds in all grade levels;
- multi-genre reading and writing;
- reading and writing workshop;
- mentor texts and exemplars, teacher models, and student samples;
- daily focus lessons and gradual-release-of-responsibility teaching;
- whole-class, independent, and book club or small-group collaborative reading;
- reader response strategies and literary analysis;
- making reading and writing connections.

Each chapter is formatted to include

- suggestions for mentor texts;
- examples of teacher models;
- samples of student work;
- activities to generate ideas and writings;
- examples of reading-like-a-writer notes, response journals, and reflections;
- Common Core State Anchor Standards addressed.

Each chapter is organized to guide teachers through the daily steps and strategies of facilitating their students' examination and writing of memoir as a genre study. The book is organized into daily lessons and details the teaching of the elements of memoir and teaching students to notice and note the attributes of effective memoirs. It demonstrates ways to teach students to read a variety of memoirs interactively, independently, collaboratively, and by means of teacher read-alouds, and describes activities and lessons that stimulate the retrieval and recording of memories and lessons that help student writers craft their own texts.

Bridging the Gap also shares approaches to implement reading and writing workshops, utilizing whole-class shared, small-group collaborative, and individual readings and writings, and model a variety of daily reading and writing activities and texts (including audiotapes, picture books, short stories, artwork, comics, excerpts, articles). Mentor texts (exemplars), teacher models, and student samples are included in the book to be shared with students.

The text points out connections with Common Core State Standards English Language Arts College and Career Readiness Standards for:

- Reading (narrative and narrative nonfiction);
- Writing (narrative and informative, as well as opportunities for opinion/argument writing or speaking);
- Speaking and Listening (as students listen to music, comedy memoir routines, hold an old-fashioned Show 'n Tell, and discuss mentor texts)
- Language.

FURTHER RATIONALE FOR READING-WRITING MEMOIRS

As memoir is an account of the writer's personal experiences built upon the memory of the writer—an exploration of a memory—memoir writing allows students to recapture moments of their pasts and, more significantly, requires that writers reflect on, and make sense of, their pasts. Adolescents need to be given opportunities to draw conclusions about the meaning and consequences of people, places, events, possessions, activities, times, crises, and decisions in their lives, and develop understandings of who they are, where they came from, and what influences contributed to their present, and possibly future, identities.

Nancie Atwell (Atwell, 1998) wrote, "Writing memoirs teaches us to recognize and explore moments on the way to growing up and becoming oneself." In that way, memoir writing also becomes inquiry-based writing and elicits critical thinking skills.

A multi-genre memoir study introduces students to a variety of reading and writing genres and makes important connections between reading and writing. Memoir writing with its many topics, perspectives, and sentiments lends itself to writing in a variety of genres, such as narratives, poetry of all types, graphic texts, scripts, brochures, news articles, speeches, and even obituaries.

Memoir writing is also housed in a variety of genres: picture books such as Cynthia Rylant's *When I Was Young in the Mountains*, poetry collections such as Rylant's *Waiting to Waltz*, poetry collections on a single topic by a variety of poets, such as John Miklos's *Grandparent Poems,* picture books based on songs lyrics such as Dolly Parton's *Coat of Many Colors*, Art Speigelman's graphic depictions of his own and his father's lives, and many songs, short essays, and novel-length writings from memoirists of all ages and cultures.

When reading memoirs as they are writing their own memoirs, readers are reading as writers, discerning and noting techniques and strategies and gaining writing skills by imitating the writers they are reading. When reading memoirs, teachers can implement the reading workshop model, and when writing memoirs, teachers can alternate with the writing workshop. Writing memoirs also affords the opportunity to study mentor texts for examples of appropriate topics and effective writing and then to apply those techniques to one's own writing.

AND . . . PREPARING FOR THE COLLEGE APPLICATION ESSAY

One additional application for memoir writing and reading in high school is to prepare students for writing the all-important college application essays. I have discovered that most students write effective and memorable college application essays once they learn how to determine (or uncover) the "writable moments" in their lives. Natural storytellers, when they find those writable moments, the words pour out and form remarkable stories communicated through skillful writing. Working on memoirs helps adolescents target those moments worth writing about and the best ways to write about them.

As the editors of *100 Successful College Application Essays, First Edition* (Georges & Georges, 1988, p. 2) disclose,

> A successful college application essay need not be produced by a gifted writer . . . we also strove more to include essays [in this book] that stood out for other reasons. And these, we believe, deserve greater attention simply because they illustrate what can be done with a little creativity and a little thought. And that, more than anything, may be what separates the average essay from the successful one.

Delsie Z. Phillips, former Director of Admissions, Haverford College, informs the college application writer (Georges, 1988, p. 11), "No matter which question, we are asking what is really important to you, who you are, and how did you arrive where you are." Memoir reading and writing gives students practice in thinking and writing about their lives and determining what is important to them and what has shaped them to become the people they have become.

RESOURCES FOR TEACHERS

This book includes a wealth of resources for classroom teachers.

- Appendix A—"Resources for Teachers" lists resources referenced in the chapters: picture books, poems and poetry collections, graphic writings, essays, collections of short memoirs, articles, artwork, and lyrics and suggested collections of memoirs that teachers could also incorporate into the unit.
- Appendix B—"Resources for Readers" contains a bibliography of more than 150 novel-length memoirs appropriate for a range and diversity of readers in grades 4–12 for student independent, small-group or book club, or whole-class memoir reading. The books were selected for diversity in reading level, interest level, topics, and cultures of the authors and include poetry collections, picture books, articles, short pieces, and novel-length books and also include memoirs—picture book, poetry collection, essay collection, and book-length—by authors of adolescent literature with whom children are familiar.

- Appendix C—"Resources for Writers" lists resources for student writers, including a bibliography of resource materials that will aid students in becoming independent writers, revisers, and editors. Appendix C also includes resources for teachers of writers.
- Appendix D— "Reproducible Forms for Readers and Writers" contains reproducible forms for writing and reading created by the author for students to use in writing memoirs and responding to reading memoirs; models of most are included within the chapter lessons.

HOW TO USE THIS BOOK

Teachers can elect which and how many activities and writings they wish to include in their curriculum. Chapters 4 through 9 contain lessons and activities for different types of memoirs, and some or all can be implemented, in any order. Teachers can introduce, and students can draft, memoirs about times, objects, people, places, events, and/or their roots. Teachers can spend time on as few as three types of memoirs or as many as all six. Writers can choose any or all drafts to take to publication through revision and editing lessons. In some classes, students worked on six drafts and chose three to take to publication in three divergent genres; in some classes we worked on three types of memoir—varied by class—and chose one to complete and publish in the most effective genre for that writing. The other drafts may be saved in portfolios or writers' notebooks for use in future revision and editing lessons.

Most important, teachers should acknowledge that not all writers wish to write about the same topics in the same mode and format, and not all writing has to be taken to final draft and graded. We all enjoy doing what we do well. Therefore, it is important to bring a sense of competence to writing, letting our writers know that they have voices and that they have something valuable to say—and that teachers are here to afford them the manner and means to do so.

WHEN TO TEACH MEMOIR WRITING

A final point is about *when* to teach memoir writing. I feel it is most effective to teach memoir writing after classroom community has been established and built, which can vary from near the beginning of the term to later in the year. Much of this writing, and accompanying activities and discussions, will be personal, and students must know and trust each other enough to share. I have experienced students writing about the day their fathers left, the day their mothers left, deaths in their families, and possessions from early childhood or from a minority or marginalized culture (ethnicity, nationality, religion).

Adolescents need to feel safe enough with each other to share artifacts of their personal pasts, their families' pasts, their cultures, their religions, their histories, or their varied circumstances. If our goal is to make their writing meaningful, all they write and talk about should be special and command respect.

However, if teachers need or wish to include memoir writing at an earlier point in the year, possibly as part of a narrative writing unit or in conjunction with a novel being taught, some of the writings and activities may be eliminated. Besides memoir writing, the purpose of this book is to present steps, strategies, and practices that are effective with teaching *all* types of writing, in any mode (type) or genre (mode), and in this way, provide a bridge to other writing and learning throughout the year.

GETTING TO THE "CORE"

Memoir reading and writing leads to reading critically and writing meaningfully to get to the "core." Adolescents reading and writing memoir discover who they are, analyze how they got there, and consider what they can become (their "core"), as well as meaningfully understanding and meeting multiple Reading, Writing, Speaking and Listening, and Language standards (the other "Core") by critiquing and constructing text. Reading and writing becomes purposeful and significant and, thereby, engages and elevates readers and writers.

I

LEARNING ABOUT MEMOIR
WRITING AND READING

DEFINING AND GATHERING MEMORIES

*A*dolescents do not spend much time reminiscing; they rarely think about their pasts or talk about memories. However, writing teachers advise them to "write what they know." And unfortunately they do; they write endlessly about going to the mall, fighting with girlfriends over boys, or trying out for the cheerleading squad or the football team or relate the saga of a fictional sports contest, point by point. What they choose to write about can be trite and clichéd. Young writers haven't yet learned that, to professional writers, these types of events are the settings—the background or catalysts—to larger plots and truths.

When writers base their stories on memories, they are writing from experience. Most authors tell us that, at least at first, their writings are based on their lives. What they seldom say, but mean, is "their *past* lives." Willa Cather wrote, "Most of the basic material a writer works with is acquired before the age of fifteen." Maybe a teacher's advice should be, "Write what you have *experienced*—and have had time to deliberate and make meaning from."

But first teachers need to help writers unleash their memories so they can choose their most writeable moments.

FREE WRITING

Free writing (see Textbox 1.1) is an effective way to inspire ideas. Writers are given a prompt and instructions that they are to write whatever the prompt inspires. They can write in any format—a personal narrative, a story in first or third person, a few paragraphs, an essay, a letter—or in no format; they can make a list or employ word association. The important thing is that writers continue to write, pen or pencil to paper, the entire time, about seven minutes. The first free write of this unit could be as simple as a phrase along the lines of "I remember . . . ."

Students write, and a few volunteers are chosen to share. If too many students volunteer to share, they can "pair-share" with a partner. In this way everyone can be heard. Many of the memories come from past days, but some surface from deep in their pasts, and teachers should point that out.

READ-ALOUD

Teacher read-aloud is an effective technique for all ages of classes, even middle and high school. Research has shown that reading aloud to students has a variety of positive learning outcomes: modeling good reading strategies and reading fluency, exposure to a variety of literature at diverse reading levels and on a variety of topics, practice in effective listening, enrichment of vocabulary, introduction of text at higher reading levels than students can read independently, opportunity for teacher think-alouds to model managing sophisticated text, and exposure to models of skilled writing, among many other benefits.

TEXT BOX 1.1.
FREE WRITING

Explanation of Free Writing: Writing anything that writers think of in response to a prompt. Writers may write directly on the subject of the prompt or may write on any topic that the prompt makes them think of. Some days some writers may want to write on their own topics. If the teachers want writers to respond directly to the prompt or on something a prompt might inspire, they should announce, "This free write will be a Focused Free Write. Please write on anything the prompt makes you think of." Writers may start to write about one topic and that may lead them to another topic.

Format of Free Writing: Writers may write in any format—story, personal narrative, poetry, letter, stream of consciousness, word association, list, essay, fiction, nonfiction, humorous, serious, written in first person, third person. . . . Writers may want to turn a free write into a finished writing at some future time.

Prompts for Free Writing: Some prompts can be more focused than others. Prompts can be phrases, excerpts from books, poetry, news articles or headlines, quotations, pictures, photographs, songs, music, artwork, picture books, maps, artifacts. . . .

Purpose of Free Writing: FLUENCY. The goal is not necessarily good writing but more writing and more ease (comfort) with writing. This is also a time for writers to take risks with their writing. Free writing also is a form of prewriting brainstorming.

Rules of Free Writing: There is only one rule to free writing: Everyone must write the entire time (even guests to the room and substitute teachers). It is very important for teachers to write—and share—along with their students. All writers should have an extra pencil or pen ready, in case. Writers need to write for the entire time, which can be about 5–8 minutes, but, if writing comes to a natural close, writers can stop there and then start up again, writing something else. Writers should not worry about spelling, grammar, or punctuation as long as the writing communicates and they can read it. Free writing should not be graded as writing. Effort points could be given.

Sharing Free Writing: Students can share their writings, a paragraph or sentence from their writings, or tell about their writings, with the entire class, in small groups, or pair share.

Teachers should only thank students for sharing. If teachers praise or discuss the writing itself ("Nice active verbs"), free writing time becomes a writing lesson, and writers become self-conscious about their writing and do not feel free to take risks.

For the first read-aloud of the unit, an appropriate choice is the picture book *Wilfrid Gordon McDonald Partridge* by Mem Fox (1992). In this book a little boy, Wilfrid Gordon McDonald Partridge, learns that Miss Nancy, a senior citizen in a neighboring old people's home, has lost her memory. He asks various people, "What's a memory?" and receives many different responses; he is told that a memory is "something warm," "something from long ago," "something that makes you cry," "something that makes you laugh," and "something as precious as gold." Wilfred uses this guidance to help Miss Nancy regain her memories.

After the story is read, class members reflect and write their answers, as a "quickwrite," to the question "What's a memory?" Everyone shares, and from those quickwrites, the class can create a "Memories Are . . ." book.

CAPTURING MEMORIES

Smell and taste are the two most effective catalysts of memories. There is a well-documented connection between smell, taste, and memory. Stuart Firestein, chair of the Department of Biological Sciences of Columbia University, refers to this as a "Proustian" experience. Even young adolescents can be introduced to Marcel Proust.

As a sensory opener, the teacher might provide madeleine cookies for the students because, first of all, many will not be acquainted with the cookie in this tale although familiarity is not necessary to the understanding of the passage, and, secondly, giving out treats gains attention and, in that way, begins the unit in a positive manner.

Due to the complexity of the passage, the first reading of this excerpt from the beginning of Marcel Proust's *Remembrance of Things Past* should be introduced through a teacher read-aloud:

And suddenly the memory returns. The taste was that of the little crumb of madeleine which on Sunday mornings at Combray (because on those mornings I did not go out before church-time), when I went to say good day to her in her bedroom, my aunt Léonie used to give me, dipping it first in her own cup of real or of lime-flower tea. The sight of the little madeleine had recalled nothing to my mind before I tasted it; perhaps because I had so often seen such things in the interval, without tasting them, on the trays in pastry-cooks' windows, that their image had dissociated itself from those Combray days to take its place among others more recent; perhaps because of those memories, so long abandoned and put out of mind, nothing now survived, everything was scattered; the forms of things, including that of the little scallop-shell of pastry, so richly sensual under its severe, religious folds, were either obliterated or had been so long dormant as to have lost the power of expansion which would have allowed them to resume their place in my consciousness. But when from a long-distant past nothing subsists, after the people are dead, after the things are broken and scattered, still, alone, more fragile, but with more vitality, more unsubstantial, more persistent, more faithful, the smell and taste of things remain poised a long time, like souls, ready to remind us, waiting and hoping for their moment, amid the ruins of all the rest; and bear unfaltering, in the tiny and almost impalpable drop of their essence, the vast structure of recollection.

And once I had recognized the taste of the crumb of madeleine soaked in her decoction of lime-flowers which my aunt used to give me (although I did not yet know and must long postpone the discovery of why this memory made me so happy) immediately the old grey house upon the street, where her room was, rose up like the scenery of a theatre to attach itself to the little pavilion, opening on to the garden, which had been built out behind it for my parents (the isolated panel which until that moment had been all that I could see); and with the house the town, from morning to night and in all weathers, the Square where I was sent before luncheon, the streets along which I used to run errands, the country roads we took when it was fine. And just as the Japanese amuse themselves by filling a porcelain bowl with water and steeping in it little crumbs of paper which until then are without character or form, but, the moment they become wet, stretch themselves and bend, take on colour and distinctive shape, become flowers or houses or people, permanent and recognisable, so in that moment all the flowers in our garden and in M. Swann's park, and the water-lilies on the Vivonne and the good folk of the village and their little dwellings and the parish church and the whole of Combray and of its surroundings, taking their proper shapes and growing solid, sprang into being, town and gardens alike, all from my cup of tea.

After reading the excerpt with the students, either the students conduct a close reading or the teacher paraphrases the content, selecting the passages and details to notice, and the class discusses how smells and tastes bring back memories. For younger students, teachers may want to merely retell the story of Mr. Proust and his cookie memories.

To engage the class and provide a sensory experience akin to Proust's, one fun suggestion is to distribute jelly beans in flavors that are most likely to evoke memories—peppermint, cotton candy, buttered popcorn, bubble gum, toasted marshmallow, red apple, cinnamon, lemon, and cherry, and request that students jot any memories triggered by the smell and then the taste.

A suggestion for the next read-aloud is Jacqueline Woodson's *Sweet, Sweet Memory* (2000). This picture book relates the story of Sarah, whose grandfather has died, and the ways she will remember him each year as she and Grandma share the corn, collards, cabbage, tomatoes, squash, and sweet potatoes from the garden he planted and have "a sweet, sweet memory." Through his garden, Grandpa will go "on and on."

The students deliberate the items and events that will help Sarah remember her grandfather and discuss the tastes of the vegetables from Grandpa's garden. In one class, Dan points out that the smells of the food cooking probably will bring back memories of the family cooking and eating together and of dinner conversations, and Amber brings up the sight of the vegetables growing and the observation that any replanting Sarah and her grandmother do will probably remind Sarah of times with her grandfather.

Classmates discuss sense memory triggers other than taste and smell—sounds, sights, and tactile experiences.

TEACHER MODEL

Aunt Es was my colorful (literally) aunt, a career woman who had obviously-dyed flaming-red hair in a time when the Clairol commercial stated, "Only [a woman's] hairdresser knows for sure." She and Uncle Nat lived in an apartment in NYC, a circumstance that filled a small-town Pennsylvania child with awe.

Uncle Sam was famous for his "Long Short Cuts." Whenever Uncle Sam said, "I know a short cut," we knew to visit the bathroom before getting into the car.

At a Thanksgiving dinner Cousin Betsy told us how she was taking Etiquette courses in college as she picked up a piece of turkey from the platter with her hands!

Donna Ward had a playhouse big enough to stand up in which made her the neighbor everyone wanted to play with. Even if someone didn't like her, everyone wanted to play with her.

The students are directed to jot down on their charts, while their teacher is sharing, if anything a story related sparks a memory for any of them. Students can then work on their charts, stopping to share a story or two with a neighbor or two, which leads to more memories to add to charts as "memories beget memories."

One additional or alternative way to capture memories, borrowed from Georgia Heard, is to provide students with a heart (Figure 1.2). Students are invited to write in the center whatever is closest to their heart, moving to the edge of the heart with people, places, and things that either are not so dear or have become less significant over the years. In the borders outside the heart, they can write what is not in their hearts. (See Appendix D, reproducible 4)

TEACHER MODEL

One teacher's example (see Figure 1.2) shows what, as a young teen, her heart may have looked like.

As the teacher completed her heart, she pointed out how her family and dog were the center of the heart, at least until she started her own family. Her next-door neighbors were as close as any relatives, closer than the actual relatives who lived a distance away. Mary Lou was her best friend in the neighborhood, and Cecilia and Marilyn at school. She loved reading; two of the series remembered were the original *Nancy Drew* and Noel Streatfield's *Shoes* books: *The Ballet Shoes, The Skating Shoes, The Ice Skating Shoes, The Circus Shoes,* and so on. Although she didn't watch a lot of television, she did have a crush on *Dr. Kildare*'s Richard Chamberlain. Mrs. C, the sixth-grade teacher, was a mean lady who paddled students at any excuse. And the teacher as an adolescent didn't like sports because she wasn't any good at playing them. As she explained and recounted her stories, students could then see why she placed her words as she did.

It is best to advise students that, during this unit, they will be adding more memories to their charts and/or hearts as they read, write, listen, and talk about memories—their own and others'. These records can lead to an endless supply of first, or third, person writings and provide topics throughout their next years (and as future authors) for memoirs, narratives, stories, and informative and, possibly, argument writings. Writers will also use diverse means to brainstorm and unleash a variety of memories later in the unit.

Figure 1.2

CCSS ELA-LITERACY ANCHOR STANDARDS ADDRESSED IN CHAPTER 1

CCSS.ELA-Literacy. CCRA. Writing 5: Develop and strengthen writing as needed by planning, revising, editing, rewriting, or trying a new approach.

FROM MEMORIES
TO MEMOIR

AN EXPLANATION OF MEMOIR

The concept of *memoir* is introduced to the students. In the past few years, "memoir" has become a term heard frequently as more and more memoirs are being written and advertised. The teacher should compare and contrast memoirs to memories by providing the definition, or explanation, that *memoir* is an account of the writer's personal experiences built on the memory of the writer. In a memoir, the writer explores the memory. There is an "I" within *memoir*.

Memoir can also be compared to autobiography. The difference between memoir and autobiography is not only that a memoir usually focuses on one event, person, place, thing, or time period, but that a memoir is not merely a recording of what happened, but an exploration of the possible *meaning* of an event, moment, or relationship. This concept can be illustrated as MEMOIR = MEMORY + REFLECTION.

The class discusses reflection—that reflection implies contemplation, a looking back, analysis, or meaning making. If teachers want a more alliterative mnemonic, they can employ the equation MEMOIR = MEMORY + MEANING MAKING.

At this point the teacher tells writers that they should focus on memories that go as far back as they can; it is best if none are more recent than two years past. Writers will need the distance or detachment of time to allow them to consider and reflect. In this unit, writers will not only reflect on where they came from, but also how those events, places, people, relationships, objects, artifacts, decisions that make up their memories served to make them who they are today.

There are numerous choices, but one example of a humorous introductory memoir to share through a read-aloud is "The Lanyard," a poem by former U.S. poet laureate Billy Collins (Collins, 2005).

In this poem Collins describes making a lanyard for his mother. The reader is aware that he is going back in time, through his memories, by his reference to "cookie nibbled by a French novelist" which students can connect with the previous introduction to Proust.

Collins's poem describes in great detail the process of making the lanyard but gives even more detail about what his mother did for him growing up and make the point that the lanyard he made as a child at summer camp was his return gift to her. The last stanza is his reflection that, looking back, he can now admit that he was sure that this craft he "wove out of boredom would be enough to make us even."

In writing the memoir and writing the reflection, students are effectively writing in two voices: the voice of their younger selves experiencing the time and topic of the memory and the voice of their present selves, looking back and reflecting.

SMALL MOMENTS

Memories are built on "small moments." It is not the people, places, times, or things; it is the small moments associated with them, the lanyard woven at camp and given as a gift. A second free-write prompt suggestion is "One time . . . " Students again write for about seven minutes and share.

A read-aloud that fits well comes from *Shelf Life*, a collection of short stories compiled by author Gary Paulsen. In his introduction to the book, Paulsen shares a moment (and person and object) that changed his life—a librarian giving him a book when he was thirteen. He explains how that first book took him over a month to finish but that the book and the ones that followed "gave [him] a life . . . that made [him] look forward instead of backward." Paulsen reflects, "I consider every good thing that has happened to me since then a result of that woman handing me that book" (p. 3). In that introduction he shares a small moment that became an influence on his future life.

A TEACHER MODEL

Teachers need to demonstrate ways writers can glean small moments from the entries on their Memories charts. For example, on her own chart one teacher listed a childhood friend. One small moment associated with that particular friend is when her older sister became engaged. The teacher shares her story.

I remember Jacie, my friend's older sister, showing us her diamond ring. That diamond was huge! I was as impressed as any little sister's friend could be. I ran home and told my father, "Jacie-Ann got engaged. She has the biggest diamond, and it's beautiful—when you look at it, it has all sorts of colors: blues, greens, pinks, yellows." My father, a jeweler, said, "It has colors because it has flaws. The flaws in the diamonds reflect light and make the colors. A flawless diamond looks pure white." I didn't care; when I became engaged, I wanted a Jacie-Ann diamond.

RECORDING SMALL-MOMENT MEMORIES

Teachers can distribute a Small Moments Chart (Tables 2.1a and 2.1b; see Appendix D, reproducibles 5 and 6) and ask students to copy one or two items from each Memories chart box and write a few key words about a small moment associated with it.

Table 2.1a. Small-Moment Memories

PERSON SMALL MOMENT	PERSON SMALL MOMENT	PERSON SMALL MOMENT	PET SMALL MOMENT
PLACE SMALL MOMENT	PLACE SMALL MOMENT	ACTIVITY SMALL MOMENT	ACTIVITY SMALL MOMENT
OBJECT SMALL MOMENT	OBJECT SMALL MOMENT	OBJECT SMALL MOMENT	TOY/GAME SMALL MOMENT
IMPORTANT EVENT SMALL MOMENT	IMPORTANT EVENT SMALL MOMENT	DECISION SMALL MOMENT	_____ SMALL MOMENT

Table 2.1b. Small-Moment Memories (page 2)

AGES/TIME				
AGE/TIME SMALL MOMENT	AGE/TIME SMALL MOMENT	AGE/TIME SMALL MOMENT	AGE/TIME SMALL MOMENT	AGE/TIME SMALL MOMENT
PHOTOGRAPH/ARTIFACT				
PHOTOGRAPH SMALL MOMENT	PHOTOGRAPH SMALL MOMENT	PHOTOGRAPH SMALL MOMENT	PHOTOGRAPH SMALL MOMENT	PHOTOGRAPH SMALL MOMENT
CRISES				
CRISIS SMALL MOMENT	CRISIS SMALL MOMENT	CRISIS SMALL MOMENT	CRISIS SMALL MOMENT	CRISIS SMALL MOMENT
Other Memories				

On his new chart under the topic "Person," Shu wrote "Tony." His small moment was the time they played basketball and he lost. One of his "Objects" was his glasses, and his small-moment memory was about the day he got his first pair of glasses. Two of Kyree's "Places" are associated with very different memories: the pet store was where he "first got a dog" and the ice cream truck that was the location of the memory of the ice cream man who gave him "an ice cream cone for free." One of his "Objects," a baseball glove, made him remember the very first time he played baseball.

CHARTING FEATURES OF A GOOD MEMOIR

At this point, writers are ready to discover what techniques and memories make a *good* memoir. To develop a class list, students listen to audiotapes of master storyteller Bill Cosby as he relates some small moments from his childhood: making and racing go-carts, playing street football, wearing sneakers with repaired soles, drinking from the refrigerator water bottle, playing Buck-Buck with Fat Albert, going to a horror movie and walking home afterward, and the more recent memory of giving his children chocolate cake for breakfast.

As they listen, the students laugh but also "notice and note what makes a good memoir." Then they can make a list of the techniques Cosby uses to create a "good" memoir. Teachers stop after each memoir or two, and students add to their Features of a Good Memoir list. One class's list read as follows:

- based on memories;
- about small moments—focuses on one thing—one race, one street football game;
- has very specific details—the music each racer used as his theme, the type of wheels for the carts—and gives names of people;
- descriptions;
- humor;

- dialogue and can hear the different voices (ways of talking) of the different speakers;
- dialect—*sumpthin'* and *outta here*;
- gives background information—audience awareness;
- topics relate to the audience's common interests and experiences;
- makes a point;
- a variety of characters included in the stories—not just the author;
- metaphors and similes;
- obvious exaggeration—hyperbole;
- onomatopoeia;
- personification;
- flashbacks;
- reflective endings.

Students continue to add to the chart during the remainder of the unit as they read or listen to more examples of memoirs from a variety of authors of different cultures written in divergent genres. Students are listening and reading like writers and drawing upon other authors as mentors. They are also employing critical thinking skills as they analyze memoirs to determine what techniques work and consider the reasons for their success.

• • •

CCSS ELA-LITERACY ANCHOR STANDARDS ADDRESSED IN CHAPTER 2

CCSS.ELA-Literacy. CCRA. Writing 5: Develop and strengthen writing as needed by planning, revising, editing, rewriting, or trying a new approach.

CCSS.ELA-Literacy. CCRA. Reading 4: Interpret words and phrases as they are used in a text, including determining technical, connotative, and figurative meanings, and analyze how specific word choices shape meaning or tone.

CCSS.ELA-Literacy. CCRA. Speaking and Listening 2: Integrate and evaluate information presented in diverse media and formats, including visually, quantitatively, and orally.

3

READING MEMOIRS
Reading Like a Writer

Adolescents read more enthusiastically and, therefore, with better comprehension, about their own interests. Of interest to adolescents are other adolescents—those similar and those different from them—or adults' stories of their adolescence, how they lived and made their decisions and the people, places, things, and events that affected them.

As students are writing memoirs, they should also be reading memoirs. They will be reading many short memoirs—picture books, poetry, song lyrics, graphics or comic strips, magazine articles, short memoir essays—in class, listening to audiotapes and read-alouds by the teacher, and reading, and analyzing, short memoir writings in small groups.

However, it is beneficial for students to also read full-length memoirs, either individually or in small groups. As they study a variety of memoir techniques and topics in class, writers can observe how published authors handle the same techniques and topics and, in that way, employ these readings as individual mentor texts. This practice teaches writers to read like writers, noticing and noting what they observe.

Memoirs are everywhere. In the past few years memoir has become one of the most popular genres, making them readily available. Memoirs have been written by comedians, television and movie stars, politicians, high-wire artists, sports figures, adventurers, models, and presidents. Appendix B contains a list of over 150 memoirs appropriate for adolescents of various ages; there are even more available for more mature readers.

Many young-adult authors with whom young adolescents are familiar, such as Gary Paulsen, Walter Dean Myers, Lois Lowry, Beverly Cleary, Jerry Spinelli, Gary Soto, Roald Dahl, and Jack Gantos, have written one or more memoirs about the different times and events in their lives; in many cases, readers can connect the ways these authors drew from their memories for their "fiction" writings. After Todd read Gary Paulsen's memoir *Guts*, he said, "Now I see where Paulsen got his ideas for *Hatchet* [a book Todd had read in sixth grade]." In addition, there are many trade memoirs written by teenagers themselves.

SCHEDULING READING WITH WRITING

An effective way to teach reading and writing is to schedule Writing Workshop three periods per week (e.g., Mondays, Wednesdays, and Fridays) and Reading Workshop for two periods per week (e.g., Tuesdays and Thursdays). To fit their schedules and administrative expectations, an alternative schedule that, out of necessity, many teachers may need to employ during this unit is to hold Writing Workshop four days per week and Reading Workshop on the remaining day. In that case, teachers may opt to have students write in class and complete independent reading as homework, allowing time in class frequently for discussions about the reading. The day(s) per week that Reading Workshop is held is a time the book clubs can meet or the teacher can support independent readers with conferencing during in-class reading.

READING MEMOIRS IN BOOK CLUBS

Some teachers may prefer that their students read memoirs in book clubs. Book clubs are small groups of students who all read a text selected by members of the group. The selection process determines the composition of the groups. Book clubs are particularly effective with adolescents because they are social and collaborative. Since each club's members plan the reading schedule, based on a specified finish date, there is peer pressure for the members to read and come to meetings prepared to share. Book club reading supports weaker readers and motivates reluctant readers. Discussion and analysis elevate proficient readers.

For book clubs to be successful, teachers need to incorporate class time for members to meet. During their meetings, readers focus their discussions on *what* the author chooses to write about (content) and *how* the author writes (organization and style). The meeting should be long enough to share journal responses and prepare a point or two to share with the class—about twenty minutes. After clubs share something from their discussion with the class, the remainder of the period can be used to independently read ahead. If teachers alternate Writing Workshop with Reading Workshop, the time for book club meetings is already built into the schedule.

Teachers can assist students in choosing the appropriate texts for book club reading by displaying five or six memoirs of which they have four or five copies each and presenting a brief book talk on each. The students have a few minutes to peruse each book; they choose a few books that interest them and read two pages to see if the reading level is appropriate and if they like the author's writing style.

Students can then note their first, second, and third choices, providing the teacher with a specific reason why they want to read each book and why they chose the books in that order. An example is Sara who wrote, "I want to read *Soul Surfer* because I heard about the girl losing her arm and want to know how she deals with it. Also I swim in the ocean when I visit my grandparents. I read a few pages and it seems to be my reading level. It is my first choice because it's about a girl and it is current and those other reasons. My second choice is . . ."

When students write down a reason for choosing a book, teachers know that the students truly are scrutinizing the book and that their decisions are based on criteria other than the fact that their friends are also considering the same book. Their responses let the teacher assess their commitment to each book and whether they actually determined that the book was at their reading and interest levels. Teachers then can form book clubs based on student choice. With three choices from each student, teachers can manipulate the composition of groups, if necessary.

One idea for memoir book clubs is to structure them around writers with whom they are familiar from their class narrative reading, such as the Lois Lowry Book Club, the Chris Crutcher Book Club, the Ralph Fletcher Book Club, and so forth. Appendix B includes memoirs that focus on the authors' childhood writing experiences.

A suggestion for more proficient readers is to organize thematic book clubs in which readers would be reading memoirs by authors in the same field, such as sports or politics, or who write about the same types of issues, such as anorexia or physical challenges, each student in the club reading a different memoir. Students would spend much of their discussions comparing and contrasting ways in which different authors write about these topics or issues.

READING MEMOIRS INDIVIDUALLY

Some teachers may prefer that students read individual titles. The advantage of students reading independently, or in pairs when warranted, is that they can choose books by a cultural diversity of memoirists (defining "culture" in its broadest sense to include ethnicity, race, gender, age, religion, sexual orientation, and intellectual and physical abilities) and by those who focus on a range of topics appealing to different readers. Individual titles also allow for a greater range in reading levels and interest levels, and students can share divergent text-based information with their classmates, thereby leading to more reading.

For classes reading individually, teachers display a collection of memoirs and conduct a "book pass." For a book pass, the teacher places one book on each desk, and each student has one minute to look at the title, read the blurb or excerpt on the back cover or inside flap, scan a page or two to ascertain the memoirist's topic and appropriateness of reading level, and note the author's style. Students then pass the books to the left. If students are certain they want to read certain books as they pass, they take the books and themselves out of the book pass.

A quicker method is small-group book passes. Students will be introduced to fewer books, but chances are that there are multiple copies of books. For ELL students, there are memoirs written in a variety of languages, longer picture book memoirs, or collections of short memoirs.

WHOLE-CLASS MEMOIR READING

While book clubs and individual reading allow for more diversity, a teacher may wish to be more familiar with the books the class is reading to better match daily reading reflections with the in-class memoir writing assignments and to support a class of reluctant readers. Those teachers can offer two or three titles, rather than only one, thereby allowing for some element of choice and diversity. Many boys do not like to read memoirs written by girls, and quite a few girls would rather not read a memoir about a boy. Some students are not interested in athletes, and some are not interested in adventurers. Most importantly, one reading level will not "fit all," no matter how homogeneous the class.

WHILE WRITERS ARE READING

To prepare for book club meetings and class discussions and to train students to read like writers, teachers should train and require students to respond in writing as they are reading. In that way, readers interact with the text as they respond to both *what* the author wrote and *how* the author wrote. Writing about what they read is the most effective way for readers to increase their comprehension. "Writing to Read," the 2009 report commissioned by the Carnegie Corporation, states that one of the core instructional practices effective in improving student reading is "Have students write about the texts they read."

Reader response is a means for readers to manipulate, explore, and challenge text. Although reader response focuses on the reader's personal interaction with the text, providing forms helps guide responders, improves and develops response, and encourages noticing and noting the author's craft.

Readers can begin with a simple two-column, double-entry, form (see Tables 3.1a and 3.1b and Appendix D, reproducibles 7 and 8).

Table 3.1a.   Memoir Double-Entry Response Journal

Quote/Information from Book	My Thoughts on **What** the Author Writes

Table 3.1b. Memoir Double-Entry Response Journal

Quote/Information from Book	My Thoughts on **How** the Author Writes

The response form consists of two columns: one for the reader to copy the writer's words directly from the text, or in some cases paraphrase, and a second column for the writer to respond to or analyze the writing.

TEACHER MODEL

It is crucial for teachers to provide response models from the memoirs that they are reading, accompanied by think-alouds that reveal their thinking as they journal. It is more advantageous for teachers to read, and give examples from, memoirs that are easy to retell so that students can follow, and it is best if they are memoirs that would engage students—either to read or to hear about. Examples from the memoir *Chinese Cinderella: The True Story of an Unwanted Daughter* by Adeline Yen Mah are included as the Teacher Model in this and following chapters.

The next step in a gradual release of responsibility lesson model would be guided practice; the students—individually or in pairs during class time—practice a journal entry based on a whole-class reading, such as the poems or picture books cited in these chapters. The students can then compare entries in small groups, and one can be chosen by each group to be shared with the class and possibly displayed as student samples for future reference.

After a week or so, some readers can progress to a more inclusive three-column format to help them respond to, and interact with, their reading and for the purposes of club or class discussion (see Table 3.3 and Appendix D, reproducible 9).

Table 3.2.

From Adeline Yen Mah's *Chinese Cinderella: The True Story of an Unwanted Daughter*	My Thoughts on **What** the Author Writes
The author tells about all the older siblings in the family and how the author's mother died in childbirth and the father remarried and then had two children with his new wife.	*I am thinking about the traditional Cinderella story. I predict that not only will the author be treated badly by her stepmother but by her siblings since she "caused" her mother's death.*
	My Thoughts on **How** the Author Writes
"She took the key from a gold chain around her neck and placed my certificate underneath her jade bracelet, pearl necklace and diamond watch, as if my award were also some precious jewel impossible to replace." (p. 2)	*As I read I notice how specific the author is. She didn't just write "expensive jewelry," she described each piece so the reader could picture it and see just how valuable the items were and how much she thought of the certificate. It was interesting that she put the certificate "underneath." It seems like she expects, or wants, it to stay there for a long time.*

Table 3.3. Memoir Triple-Column Response Journal

What the Author Wrote (Quote/Information)	My Thoughts	What I Might Try in My Writing

Table 3.4.

What the Author Wrote (About)	My Thoughts	What I Might Try in My Writing
Mah's grandmother describes the Chinese custom of foot binding in great detail (pp. 7–8)	By the way it's written, I can tell that Nai Nai, the grandmother, doesn't believe this was a good custom and is glad for her granddaughter that "this horrible custom was done away with thirty years ago."	I might write a memoir about some customs that were in our family that we no longer follow, such as marriages arranged by the family, as well as some customs that we still hand down, and some that we made up, like wearing scarabs on every Friday the 13.

Journaling demonstrates how students are reading and comprehending and reflecting on their reading as formative assessment for the teacher, as well as providing examples of techniques for writers to try in their own writing.

Each of the following chapters contains ideas and instructions for students to read as writers while they are writing different types of memoirs.

• • •

CCSS ELA-LITERACY ANCHOR STANDARDS ADDRESSED IN CHAPTER 3

CCSS.ELA-Literacy. CCRA. Writing 9: Draw evidence from literary or informational texts to support analysis, reflection, and research.

CCSS.ELA-Literacy. CCRA. Reading 1: Read closely to determine what the text says explicitly and to make logical inferences from it; cite specific textual evidence when writing or speaking to support conclusions drawn from the text.

CCSS.ELA-Literacy. CCRA. Reading 2: Determine central ideas or themes of a text and analyze their development; summarize the key supporting details and ideas.

CCSS.ELA-Literacy. CCRA. Reading 3: Analyze how and why individuals, events, or ideas develop and interact over the course of a text.

CCSS.ELA-Literacy. CCRA. Reading 4: Interpret words and phrases as they are used in a text, including determining technical, connotative, and figurative meanings, and analyze how specific word choices shape meaning or tone.

CCSS.ELA-Literacy. CCRA. Reading 5: Analyze the structure of texts, including how specific sentences, paragraphs, and larger portions of the text (e.g., a section, chapter, scene, or stanza) relate to each other and the whole.

CCSS.ELA-Literacy. CCRA. Reading 6: Assess how point of view or purpose shapes the content and style of a text.

CCSS.ELA-Literacy. CCRA. Reading 9: Analyze how two or more texts address similar themes or topics in order to build knowledge or to compare the approaches the authors take.

CCSS.ELA-Literacy. CCRA. Reading 10: Read and comprehend complex literary and informational texts independently and proficiently.

II

DRAFTING DIVERSE MEMOIRS

as it does today,
all the dark blue speed drained out of it.

This is the beginning of sadness, I say to myself,
as I walk through the universe in my sneakers.
It is time to say good-bye to my imaginary friends,
time to turn the first big number.

It seems only yesterday I used to believe
there was nothing under my skin but light.
If you cut me I could shine.
But now when I fall upon the sidewalks of life,
I skin my knees. I bleed.

Although with a dramatic reading of the poem, adolescents usually laugh over Collins's "beginning of sadness"; they then begin to think about how it feels to get older. They become nostalgic for their youth, and they commiserate with Collins over losing childish imagination and make-believe. Young Billy was an Arabian wizard, a soldier, a prince; he had imaginary friends and could make himself invisible by employing his own magical personal ritual. The class will have already discussed that memoirs contain reflections on the past, and now students will notice that Collins ends his poem with a reflection about life now that he is ten and the magic is receding and just what that means.

Students can begin sharing stories of their past imaginary friends—an almost universal experience—and guilelessly dressing up and role-playing with no embarrassment or awkwardness. In one class a student shares how she always went to the mall in her princess dress; another outdoes that with stories about the tutu she wore *everywhere*, even to school. The boys had been pirates, and one was sure that Cookie Monster lived in his house, somewhere.

BRAINSTORMING IDEAS

The students each draft a timeline or time-graph (a timeline with pictures or drawings) to brainstorm these memories (see Table 4.1). Sometimes this is referred to as a "graphic life map" although life maps are not necessarily drawn chronologically.

Table 4.1. Memory Time-Graph

In each box, chronologically draw pictures of memories of certain ages. The furthest left side of each column is your birth date.

	Year I Was Born	Year I Was 1	Year I Was 2	Year I Was 3	Year I Was 4	Year I Was 5	Year I Was 6	Year I Was 7
Birthday								
3 months								
6 months								
9 months								

Students can relocate memories from their other charts, but since many of those memories crossed years, they can use the timeline for memories exclusive to certain ages or change in age. Some of these memories may later be used in their "crises" memoirs (see Chapter 8).

TEACHER MODEL

As a model, teachers fill out their own charts: moved into new house at age two; adopted dog at age three; Florida vacation for fourth birthday; a cat at age six; just after turning twelve, sister left for college. . . .

A different type of chart might be a Pros & Cons Chart (see Table 4.2 and Appendix D, reproducible 11) based on a certain birthday.

Table 4.2. Pros & Cons Charts of Turning _____

PROS	CONS

TEACHER MODEL

One teacher charted turning sixteen.

Table 4.3.

PROS	CONS
Driver's License; Metallic Green LeManns	Job—less free time
Could try out for cheerleader or majorette	Need to start looking for colleges
Can be a Counselor-in-Training at summer camp	Too old to be a camper
	Junior in H.S.—more difficult courses

As the next step, the teacher drafted a poem, "Sweet Sixteen," with the assistance of her chart. She opted to try a free-verse poem, modeled loosely on Mr. Collins's poem as a mentor text, and thought aloud as she made decisions, drafted, and took suggestions from the class.

It's "That" summer.
I am turning sixteen.
"Sweet Sixteen" some call it.
The occasion is marked by a party.

This is the beginning of my new Life.
I pass my driver's test—
     On my third try.
(Luckily, I didn't strike out.)
Accompanied by Responsibilities, like buying gas.
     This leads to a job—local library.
My free time gone.
My childhood over.

The students point to comments about school, and the teacher adds items from the chart and items that the writing and think-aloud invokes:

This is the beginning of a new Era.
Advanced courses,
     Planning for college.
A chance to try out for Cheerleader or Majorette
     And represent my high school. I do.
     Less free time.

What is gone? Merriment and Play and Time—forever.
I have entered the Big Leagues.
     Everything counts
     For the rest of my life.

What is gained?
    Maturity. Responsibility.
What was lost?
    Innocence. Lightheartedness. Childhood.

The poem is truly a rough draft, and the teacher hasn't used everything on the chart, but the activity gets the class started. The students listen to the think-alouds and observe the decision-making process; the teacher now has something to work with, along with the students, as teachers should write with their students.

ANOTHER MENTOR TEXT

Teachers should always endeavor to give students choices. Choice is a powerful motivator. Many studies have been conducted on the effect of choice. Results of forty-one studies on "the effect of choice on intrinsic motivation and related outcomes in a variety of settings with both child and adult samples indicated that providing choice enhanced intrinsic motivation, effort, task performance, and perceived competence, among other outcomes" (http://www.ncbi.nlm.nih .gov/pubmed/18298272).

Therefore, teachers should share another, different poem that focuses on a grade in the author's life, such as Mark Vinz's "What I Remember About the 6th Grade" (Vinz, 1992).

We lost the school softball championship
when that four-eyed kid popped out
with the bases loaded. We did win the
spelling bee, though. Weird Charlie said
It was because we had the ugliest girls.

The Scarlet Tanager edged out the Wood Duck
in our balloting for the State Bird
because the girls liked red and organized.
I voted for the Bluejay or maybe the Loon.
Weird Charlie voted for the Crow.

The teacher nearly got knocked cold when
a big picture of George Washington or somebody
fell off the wall and conked her on the head.
Most of the girls cried. Most of the boys
laughed, especially Weird Charlie.

Once a month or so they'd herd us
to the basement for atomic bomb drills
and films of houses exploding in firestorms.
When it came to the Nuclear Age,
even Weird Charlie kept his mouth shut.

The teacher distributes copies, and together the students annotate the poem, identifying Mr. Vinz's ideas. One class's annotations:

We lost the school softball championship —*sports competition—something bad that happened*
when that four-eyed kid popped out —*class nerd; can't remember name; maybe nickname*
with the bases loaded. We did win the —*something good that happened; class statistics*
spelling bee, though. Weird Charlie said —*every class has someone who is/seems "different"*
It was because we had the ugliest girls. —*stereotyping*

The Scarlet Tanager edged out the Wood Duck
in our balloting for the State Bird —*class activity-lesson; contest participation*
because the girls liked red and organized. —*girls in class*
I voted for the Bluejay or maybe the Loon.
Weird Charlie voted for the Crow.

The teacher nearly got knocked cold when —*story about teacher*
a big picture of George Washington or somebody
fell off the wall and conked her on the head.
Most of the girls cried. Most of the boys —*girls' reaction vs boys' reaction*
laughed, especially Weird Charlie. —*Weird Charlie POV story*

Once a month or so they'd herd us
to the basement for atomic bomb drills
and films of houses exploding in firestorms. —*fears; rituals; history*
When it came to the Nuclear Age,
even Weird Charlie kept his mouth shut. —*reflection based on Weird Charlie's reaction*

TEACHER MODEL

Students listen and watch as the teacher creates a chart of memories from one of her most memorable grades, third grade, thinking aloud so that the students see *and* hear her thought process.

- *Mrs. Johnston, my favorite elementary school teacher*
- *my sister went to high school and no longer accompanied me to school; no more walking me to the bus stop, stopping on Wilmont Lane to pick up her two friends, tall girls with the long ponytails, one blonde, one brunette (and my sister a redhead)*
- *going to school with friends from the neighborhood*
- *class trip—maple sugaring*
- *cooking down and tasting maple sugar*
- *Girls didn't play sports, but on the playground we jumped rope and played jacks*
- *I could get to sixzies on a first try*
- *Janie Ward got all the way to tenzies one time*
- *Jeanie M, the tiniest girl in the third grade*
- *the baby alligator that someone brought to our class*
- *the death and burial of the baby alligator*
- *best friends Cecilia and Patty*
- *"real" math*
- *Our "Weird Charlie," the kid who walked around during class and pulled on ponytails*

The teacher next highlights those items that will lead to her reflection. She considers what, besides a favorite teacher, made that grade, of all the grades of school, most memorable. As she continues to think aloud, her thoughts focus on the alligator story and the fact that she was no longer the "little sister" going to school with her big sister's protection. She determines that even though only eight years old, it was a growing-up grade of sorts—forced independence and a first experience with death. That became the focus of the reflection.

What I Remember About the 3rd Grade (modeled after Mark Vinz)

My sister went off to high school and
I walked all the way to the bus stop myself,
No longer accompanied by the tall blonde, brunette, and redhead
But by friends from the neighborhood—
Cathy, Cindy, and Roslyn Jane.

We had our favorite teacher, Mrs. Johnson who
Took us out in the woods maple sugaring.
We came back to the classroom and
Cooked the syrup down, down to a few tablespoons of
Maple sugar. There wasn't enough for me to taste.

Someone gave our class a baby alligator.
It was eight inches long, not scary at all.
We named him Allie and took turns looking in his bowl.
Allie died within a few weeks, and we buried him in front of the school,
I helped make a cross for his grave even though I was Jewish.

This was the year of the recess Jacks Competitions. I was one of the
Champions , reaching sixzies on one turn.
Jeanie Ward made it all the way to tenzies one time and was
Titleholder of the Playground—at least on the girls' side.
Boys played on the other side, in the grass, still saying girls had cooties.

In third grade at the age of eight, I made friends whom
I would keep through high school. I learned about
"real" math—not just adding and subtracting, and
independence, disappointment, and death. But I
really didn't believe I had cooties, just that boys were stupid.

It is very important that students first analyze and deconstruct a mentor text but then observe their teachers' reconstruction processes as they create their own version, thinking aloud as they do so and involving the class when possible. This crucial part of the process separates "teaching writing" from "assigning writing."

This process need not be completed prior to student drafting each time. As students add to their lists or charts of memories or highlight items that they have already brainstormed that define a particular age or grade, teachers can draft a stanza or two of their writings on a document projector or Smartboard so that writers can observe the process. Students can see that some items are included in the draft and others (Jeanie M) are not, that details (eight inches, cooties, not getting to taste the maple sugar) can be added during the drafting process, and that authors experiment with line breaks when writing free verse.

Those who need the support to write their own texts watch, and follow, the teacher more closely; those more confident or those who have enough of their own ideas begin their rough drafts, glancing up from time to time to observe the teacher's progress. They note the countless changes, cross-outs, and caret-ins and how words and ideas move around with arrows in the "Sloppy Copy."

Teachers need not be concerned that they think of themselves as accomplished writers. They are modeling the process, not the product. There are enough mentor texts that can be used as exemplars.

YET ANOTHER MENTOR TEXT

For developing or reluctant writers, teachers may introduce the list poem in place of the Vinz poem. A list poem is one of the simplest types of poetry to write; it is simply a list of things and can be written in free verse or rhyme. Two mentor texts are the simple structure, but challenging text, of two William Stafford poems, "What's in My Journal" (Stafford, 1998) and "What I Learned Last Week" (Stafford, 2014).

After discussing the poems, the class can brainstorm ways they can imitate them or use one of them as a mentor text to write their own list poem that reveals life at a certain age or period of life. Samples of topics students have brainstormed are:

What Was in My _____ Grade Journal.
What Was in My _____ Grade Cubby/Locker.
What Was in My ____-Year-Old Heart.
What Was under My ____-Year-Old Bed.
What Was in my Childhood Toybox.
Things I Learned in _____ Grade.
Things I Learned as a Baby, . . . at Age ____.
Things I Lost When I Was ____ Years Old.

CREATING A TEACHER MODEL

To demonstrate, a Teacher Model can be created using the previous third-grade list, thinking aloud, and enlisting the help of the class.

What I Learned in Third Grade by Mrs. R

Alligators, when they live in grade school classrooms,
don't live very long.

Eight-year-olds can walk to the bus stop
on their own.

When you cook down maple syrup into sugar,
you learn that you didn't gather enough.

Sometimes it's fun to be a girl, jumping rope and playing jacks
instead of running around the playground and knocking each other down,
like a stupid third-grade boy.

If I practice really hard at jacks,
I can get to sixies on the first try

which is a Big Deal for me,
even though Janie Ward got to tenzies once.

In first and second grade I was the smallest;
in third grade Jeanie M was the tiniest girl in the grade.
At Patten Grade School, the best teacher
is Mrs. Johnson, and third grade is the best year
with best friends, triumphs, one tragedy (Allie), and real math,
Even looking back on it from the future.

For students who do not elect to draw on the list-poem format for this particular memoir, the structures can be employed for memoirs about people (Chapter 6):

- "Things I Learned from My Grandparents"
- "Things I Learned from My Friends/Adversaries"
- "Things I Learned from Uncle Leo"
- "Things I Learned from Family Albums"

or about places (Chapter 7):

- "What Was in My Childhood Neighborhood"
- "What Was in My Bedroom"
- "Things I Learned in My Backyard"
- "Things I Learned at Summer Camp"

or crises (chapter 8):

- "Things I Learned about Divorce"
- "Things I Learned from Breaking My Leg"
- "Things I Learned from My First Swim Meet"
- "Things I Learned from Running Away from Home at 5"

After students finish their drafts, they place them in their writing folders. During this unit, students draft a variety of writings; later they will choose the one, two, or three to take to publication.

One suggestion is to have three folders in a hanging folder for each student. "Seeds" is the ideas folder where all the charts and lists reside; "Seedlings" houses the drafts; and "Plants" is the folder that contains their final published writings. A Writer's Notebook can also be divided into the same three sections, along with a "Lessons" section.

STUDENT SAMPLE

Debbie (pseudonym), age thirteen, drew upon the Billy Collins model and wrote "Double Digits."

I wake up and everything looks the same;
It's not the same though.

My father asks me how I feel;
I shrug my shoulders.
I can't describe how I feel.
I'm no longer the same now;
I am a double digit

I used to be carefree;
I was a single number.
Now I have responsibilities;
I am a double digit

My friends say its no big change;
They say they all feel the same.
But I feel different;
For now I'm a double digit.

As I blow out the candles,
I wish I could go back
To the land of single numbers,
But I am now a double digit.

READING LIKE WRITERS

As the class brainstorms and drafts time, age, or grade memoirs, students are reading their memoir books, each noticing ways in which the author might have used the techniques they are attempting as well as techniques they may wish to try. In that way the full-length memoirs also serve as mentor texts. Readers are asked to notice what ages or time periods appear to be especially memorable or important to their writer and note how they, as readers, are aware of this significance. An example comes from the memoir *Chinese Cinderella: The True Story of an Unwanted Daughter* by Adeline Yen Mah (Mah, 1999). Based on reading the memoir, it appears that one of Adeline's most memorable years is when she is in fifth form and wins an international playwriting competition. This format is a simplified version of the double-entry journal in Chapter 3 that teachers can use to begin, if necessary.

Table 4.4.

Quote/Information from Book	My Thoughts
Adeline finishes her last year of boarding school and wins an international playwriting contest. Because of this, her father allows her to go to England to college (pp.190–92).	I thought the author makes this scene *suspenseful*. When Adeline is summoned home, she thinks that she will not even be able to finish her school year and dreads the future so I was sure she was about to experience more abuse, but her father has brought her home to congratulate her. The way the author wrote it, I felt her surprise. Her father then does agree to let her to go to England although he tells her that she has to study medicine, *which keeps him in character*. It would seem unusual if he agreed to her wishes to study writing.
Adeline's father bought her home to congratulate her because the news that she won a contest gave him "face" in front of an important colleague (" . . . I had given him face.")	The author brought in the fact the colleague was the one who saw the news in the paper. I think this illustrated how her father had to be shown how valuable his daughter was. I also notice that the author is always weaving in information about Chinese culture.

The same passages are reflected in the double-entry response form introduced in Chapter 3.

After reading like writers, readers are aware of techniques they can try and embed them in their own writings.

Table 4.5.

From Adeline Yen Mah's *Chinese Cinderella: The True Story of an Unwanted Daughter*	My Thoughts on **What** the Author Writes
Adeline finishes her last year of boarding school and wins an international playwriting contest. Because of this, her father allows her to go to England to college (pp.190–92).	When Adeline is summoned home, she thinks that she will not even be able to finish her school year and dreads the future so I was sure she was about to experience more abuse, but her father has brought her home to congratulate her. Her father then does agree to let her to go to England to college.
	My Thoughts on **How** the Author Writes
	1) The author makes this scene suspenseful by beginning it with a review of all the bad things that had happened and that coming was "perhaps the end of school forever" and an arranged marriage, Adeline's biggest fear. And the scene takes place in Father's room, a "place to which [she] had never been invited." 2) She writes that Father agrees she can go to college but tells her that she has to study medicine instead of writing, *which keeps him in character.*

• • •

CCSS ELA-LITERACY ANCHOR STANDARDS ADDRESSED IN CHAPTER 4

CCSS.ELA-Literacy. CCRA. Writing 2: Write informative/explanatory texts to examine and convey complex ideas and information clearly and accurately through the effective selection, organization, and analysis of content.

CCSS.ELA-Literacy. CCRA. Writing 3: Write narratives to develop real or imagined experiences or events using effective technique, well-chosen details and well-structured event sequences.

CCSS.ELA-Literacy. CCRA. Writing 4: Produce clear and coherent writing in which the development, organization, and style are appropriate to task, purpose, and audience.

CCSS.ELA-Literacy. CCRA. Writing 5: Develop and strengthen writing as needed by planning, revising, editing, rewriting, or trying a new approach.

CCSS.ELA-Literacy. CCRA. Writing 9: Draw evidence from literary or informational texts to support analysis, reflection, and research.

CCSS.ELA-Literacy. CCRA. Writing 10: Write routinely over extended time frames (time for research, reflection, and revision) and shorter time frames (a single sitting or a day or two) for a range of tasks, purposes, and audiences.

CCSS.ELA-Literacy. CCRA. Reading 4: Interpret words and phrases as they are used in a text, including determining technical, connotative, and figurative meanings, and analyze how specific word choices shape meaning or tone.

CCSS.ELA-Literacy. CCRA. Reading 5: Analyze the structure of texts, including how specific sentences, paragraphs, and larger portions of the text (e.g., a section, chapter, scene, or stanza) relate to each other and the whole.

CCSS.ELA-Literacy. CCRA. Reading 6: Assess how point of view or purpose shapes the content and style of a text.

5

MEMOIRS OF
OBJECTS AND MEMENTOES

Writing about items, belongings, or keepsakes seems to lend itself to some of the most varied writing in topics, tone, and format of any of the types of adolescent memoirs. A prized possession can be a stuffed animal, a piece of blanket, a family heirloom, an award, a toy, an outfit, or even a house.

MENTOR TEXTS

There are so many choices of published memoirs about possessions to share that it is difficult to know where to start. Teachers can begin with Dolly Parton's familiar song "Coat of Many Colors," playing a version of Ms. Parton singing her song based on her childhood memories, either on YouTube or on a CD. At the same time, students can follow along with her picture book of the same title, viewing the lyrics and the illustrations.

After students discuss possessions they have had, adding to their Memories chart, the teacher can read *The Keeping Quilt,* one of Patricia Polacco's picture-book memoirs (1998). This book shares the story of a quilt that Ms. Polacco's great-great-grandmother made from the clothes her family wore when they immigrated to America from Russia. She made the quilt from Polacco's Great-Gramma Anna's dress and *babushka* and from other relatives' shirt, nightdress, and apron. Through the generations, the quilt was handed down and used as a tablecloth, a baby blanket for many of the children born, and a play tent.

But most importantly, it was used as a wedding *huppa* for Anna, her daughter Carle, Carle's daughter Mary Ellen, and finally Patricia herself. As the author describes these weddings, she describes the Jewish traditions and how some traditions remained the same and others changed over the years. "After [Anna and Sasha's] wedding, the men and women celebrated separately," and at Carle and George's wedding "Men and women celebrated together, but they still did not dance together," but at Mary Ellen's wedding "For the first time, friends who were not Jews came to the wedding." Last, "At [Patricia's] wedding to Enzo-Mario, men and women danced together." The book ends with the reflection that Patricia and her husband's daughter Traci Denise, "Someday . . . will leave home and she will take the quilt with her."

The students conduct a conversation about the topic of the memoir—the quilt. The book is printed in sepia tones, with brown text; the quilt stands out as the only colored illustration in the book. Students discuss the effectiveness of this technique and ways this technique could be translated into writing. The students share opinions such as, "The object could be typed in a different font." "The object could be typed in color." "A picture of the object could be included every time the object is mentioned or at the top of every page."

More significant, students discuss what, besides the object, the memoir is about and how this is reflected in the ending. Most students come up with such answers as "family," traditions," "customs," "ancestors," "culture or religion," and "an object that has become an heirloom." One student discussed how the object let the author tell about "many small moments and how those moments related through the quilt." As precious as the quilt is, students always realize that the story was about more than the quilt, an observation that can make their reading and writing richer.

This conversation will take the discussion back to *Coat of Many Colors* and leads into small-group discussions about the significance of the coat and the reasons a famous, wealthy country singer may choose to write and sing about it.

Another point that can be raised is that the item or possession that is memorable does not need to belong to the memoirist. An example is "Sandy's Toy Bin," a poem written by one of Nancie Atwell's students (Atwell, 2002). In the poem Ashley writes about her dog's toy bin and how the toys belong to her dog, but the "memories are mine." Students find this concept interesting and take time to think about something that belongs to someone else that holds memories from them and to share these stories with a partner—and then add these items to one of their memory-capturing charts.

SHOW 'N TELL

An "Old-Fashioned Show 'n Tell" can be scheduled for the next day. Students should be given a week's notice to locate an item that is particularly meaningful in their past to bring for a Show 'n Tell ("Nothing that breathes"). As adolescents, it will have been some years since their last such experience, and they usually appear intrigued.

When Show 'n Tell day arrives, students walk in carting all sorts of items, big and small. This is one reason it is important to have built a safe, respectful community, as these keepsakes and their owners can be quite unusual and need to be treated with respect.

READ-ALOUD

Class begins with a read-aloud. In Roald Dahl's first memoir, *Boy: Tales of Childhood* (1986), the author gives an account of his daily visits with his friends to the sweetshop. They would stop on their way to and from school where they would gaze through the windows. "Each of us received a sixpence a week for pocket-money and whenever there was any money in our pockets, we would troop in together to buy a pennyworth of this or that" (p. 29). In this part of the memoir Dahl describes his obsession with Gobstoppers, curious about how they changed color. "There was something fascinating about the way it went from pink to blue to green to yellow" (p. 32). Students familiar with *Charlie & the Chocolate Factory*, either the book or the movies, are amazed that Dahl's novel was created from his own experiences and memories.

TEACHER MODEL

Based on Dahl's account, the teacher shares his Show 'n Tell item—Fireballs candy. He talks about penny candy, describing trips to the penny-candy store and the glass-front case situated at the front of the store and filled with Fireballs, Mary Janes, Pixie Sticks, Candy Lipsticks, Licorice Whips and Licorice Wheels, Wax Lips, Bit O' Honey, Caramel Creams, Tootsie Rolls, Wax Bottles, Jaw Breakers, and Candy Buttons. He relates the power and pride of being a consumer and having all the rights that role entailed even if one only had a penny or two. His childhood town was not affluent, but every child could scare up a penny, which allotted unlimited browsing and choosing time for the agonizing decisions made in front of that case. Penny candy represented more than just candy; it represented childhood and a little bit of choice and power.

Cynthia Rylant's poem "Wax Lips" (2001) shares the same experience. Ms. Rylant remembers specific details of her store in Beaver—that it was a hardware store (Todd's Hardware) and some of the items that were sold there were nails and lawnmowers—probably because the candy counter was located in the back and the kids had to walk through the store to get to the candy counter, which also may have been why Mrs. Todd was "white-faced and silent." She also remembers wax lips, Mary Janes, and sugar straws.

Teachers can bring in any items, accompanied by appropriate stories and mentor texts, to share.

STUDENTS MEMENTO SHARE: IN SHOW 'N TELL

When the students enter the classroom, their desks should be arranged in groups of four or five, and they can be invited to "sit anywhere." It is especially important that students are comfortable because they are truly sharing a part of their lives. If the year is spent building community and working on promoting peer respect (Roessing, 2012), students generally will feel comfortable to sit wherever convenient, not worrying about with whom they are sitting.

As they sit in their small groups, they take turns sharing, following the teacher's example. Instructions are, "In groups of five, share your memento, one at a time, everyone *listening* to the storyteller.

Tell about your memento—

1. What it is.
2. Where it came from and/or how you got it.
3. Why it is memorable and special.
4. Share <u>one</u> story (small moment) about your object.
5. Be respectful of each other's keepsakes and stories."

Students then introduce their objects, recount small moments associated with them, and discuss the mementoes' importance in their past and the role the items have played in making them who they are.

In most classes it is typical that several girls *and boys* have pieces of baby blankets, stuffed animals, and well-worn dolls. There are a plethora of award ribbons and trophies, and some bring articles of clothing or jewelry. Some bring toys; the boys unself-consciously commence playing with one young man's Fisher-Price Pirate Ship and share stories of owning the same pirate ship. Many students have artifacts from distant countries, times, cultures, and religions. Some items have monetary value, and some have merely emotional value. A few are even homemade, as Billy Collins's lanyard was. Some, like Amanda's bear, have been passed down from mother to daughter.

Writers keep their Memories charts available so they can add memories generated by others' items and stories. They are asked to leave their objects, take them home and bring back the next class, or take a good picture to bring to their next class.

WRITING ODES ABOUT OBJECTS

One goal of this memoir unit is to expose students to different types of writing and have them attempt divergent types without necessitating a "commitment" to any. In other words, writers try new forms as rough drafts but then have the option, as writers, to make any changes for a final draft or even in a second rough draft. There is no penalty for taking risks. At this point, writers acquire credit for the effort, not a grade for the product.

This writing—an object memoir—lends itself to teaching odes. The three characteristics of an ode are explained. It

- focuses on one object;
- contains elaborate description; and
- is celebratory or even glorifying in tone.

MENTOR TEXTS

The teacher can distribute, and read with the class, some odes by Chilean poet Pablo Neruda. One of Neruda's odes that is fun to include is "Ode to the Tomato" (1990). Students always find this ode in particular to entertainingly and humorously fit the characteristics of an ode, its descriptions being effusive as Neruda celebrates the tomato as "star of earth." Even young students understand the excessive, over-the-top, elaborate descriptions and glorifying tone when read aloud, the reader emphasizing and acting out parts.

In pairs, the students highlight any descriptive words and phrases. In a second highlighter color, they highlight words and phrases that foster a celebratory, festive, or praising tone.

The odes of Pablo Neruda are available in Spanish and when classes include native Spanish-speaking ELL students, both versions of poems can be distributed and read.

Easier for younger students to follow as their mentor text is Gary Soto's tribute, "Ode to Pablo's Tennis Shoes."

They wait under Pablo's bed,
Rain-beaten, sun-beaten,
A scuff of green at their tips
From when he fell
In the school yard.
He fell leaping for a football
That sailed his way.
But Pablo fell and got up,
Green on his shoes,
With the football
Out of reach.

Now it's night.
Pablo is in bed listening
To his mother laughing
To the Mexican novelas on TV.
His, shoes, twin pets,
That snuggle his toes,
Are under the bed.
He should have bathed,
But he didn't.
(Dirt rolls from his palm,
Blades of grass
Tumble from his hair.)
He wants to be
Like his shoes,
A little dirty
From the road,
A little worn
From racing to the drinking fountain
A hundred times in one day.
It take water
To make him go.
And his shoes to get him
There. He loves his shoes,
Cloth like a sail,
Rubber like
A lifeboat on rough sea.
Pablo is tired,

Sinking into the mattress.
His eyes sting from
Grass and long words in books.
He needs eight hours
Of sleep
To cool his shoes,
The tongues hanging
Out, exhausted.

The students conduct a close reading of the ode, looking for, and noting, then sharing, the attributes that would cause Soto to call it an ode: one special object; elaborate, detailed description; and a laudatory tone. The writing focuses only on Pablo's tennis shoes, "twin pets." Some of the descriptive words students identify in this ode are "rain-beaten," "sun-beaten," "green at their tips," "a little dirty," "a little worn," "cloth," and "rubber."

They note as celebratory ideas the portrayal of the shoes as "pets," the fact they "snuggle his toes" and that Pablo even "wants to be like his shoes." These special shoes get him where he needs to go "like a sail, "and are "like a lifeboat on rough seas." The poet even states that "He *loves* his shoes" and declares that Pablo's need for sleep is for his shoes to have time "to cool," presumably so he can wear them again.

Soto intersperses Spanish words and phrases, including a glossary in *Neighborhood Odes*. This allows students from Spanish-speaking cultures to incorporate this techniques in their writings (see Chapter 9).

TEACHER MODEL

The students draft odes to their objects. But before students look at their charts to choose a topic and begin their drafts, a teacher model, such as "Ode to My Passport," can be shared.

Ode to My Passport

Little indigo blue book.
Color of the night sky through which I fly,
Over Oceans to distant Lands and even
Worlds.
Pages filled with stamps,
Evidence, Proof, Testimony, Confirmation
Of my travels,
Allowing me to transcend boundaries –
Both literal and figurative.

Because of you, I have
    Grown,
    Expanded
    My own
    Boundaries.
I am now a World Traveler!

Three by five inches of pure Adventure,
And only one-half inch thick,

You are
Twenty-five pages of Exploration, Discovery.
Smells of exotic spices
And foreign Intrigue.

Scotland, where my education began,
Glasgow to St. Andrews to Edinburgh.
Italy, my passion, from the cities to the small hill towns,
From Sicily to Sardinia.

Paris, romance;
Seville, longevity;
Budapest, resilience,
Vienna, Gibraltar, London, and places
I have not yet seen.

With me since childhood
Leading me to journeys—to other Lands
To other Lives.
Without you, I might have been,
Would have been,
Less.

With you at my side, I am confident,
a Citizen of the World,
a Seeker of the Unique.
Passport, you are my constant guide to
Cultures,
Places,
People.

As your pages fill with stamps
In colors of the rainbow,
So does my heart.
I learn Tolerance,
Understanding,
Acceptance,
For others and myself.

Passport, you have been with me all along.
Only you have made this journey possible.
With you, as each page turns,
So does my life.
With each renewed passport,
A new chapter unfolds, and I am renewed
And reinvented.

The Ode to the Ring by Nicole Brestowski

Stunning,
Gleaming,
The ring grasps my finger.
A perfect look.
A perfect fit.
A ruby sits
In the middle
With
Shiny gold
Hands keeping it in place.
Suffocated
By diamonds,
Armies of soldiers;
Twelve
Sparkling
Rocks.
All banded to
Gold
To form
A
Ring.

A real treasure
Never awkward or displaced,
At least
Within the
Tat-tat of my heart.
Power, forcefulness,
You are majestic.
With
You
I am
Fearless.

No
Bracelet,
Necklace,
Or assortment of
Brooches
Can outshine you
And your
Intrinsic beauty;
The things

You represent
To
Me.

I am often taken
Back
To a time
Where the days
Are filled
With memories.
Some of my mom
And the day
You were gifted to me.

Other
Memories as well.
Most good but some
Bad.
All important.
All necessary.
All sentimental.
These
Have shaped
Me into whom
And what
I am today.

You will always be with me.
Experiencing
New things,
Together,
United
Like the states.

I
Know
Where to find
You.
Where you
Have been
And
Will be,
Upon
My finger.

Figure 5.1.

Ode to Baseball by Andrew Karahalis

The field
Filled with players.
Afternoon.
Summer.
Children strive
To be like
Their
Baseball heroes .
Their homeruns
Sail
Through the alleys.

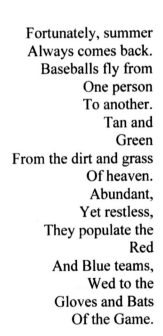

In December,
Resting,
The baseballs
Have nothing
To do.
They sit in a
Glove,
Waiting eagerly
For someone
To send it sailing
Through the air.

Fortunately, summer
Always comes back.
Baseballs fly from
One person
To another.
Tan and
Green
From the dirt and grass
Of heaven.
Abundant,
Yet restless,
They populate the
Red
And Blue teams,
Wed to the
Gloves and Bats
Of the Game.

Figure 5.2.

The teacher describes the creation process. First a topic is determined based on something of value to the author that also has associated memories. This can be decided by referring to the Memories and Heart charts. On this writer's Heart chart (see Chapter 1) was the term "travel." Something that means a lot to her is traveling, especially to foreign places.

She shares her thought process: *Now, what possessions do I have that relate to travel? I do have some artifacts from different travels, but not from all of them. When I went to college in Scotland, I only brought back photographs and memories. I have some artifacts from my travels to Italy. I don't do a lot of shopping when I travel, and no one artifact reminds me of ALL my travel.*

Then it comes to me. There is one possession that has been with me on all my travels—my passport. It hasn't been the same passport—they have to be renewed—but they all represent the same thing, travel. So I will write about my passport.

The next step is developing the description. I stare at my passport. Navy blue. I want to be more precise so I check The Describer's Dictionary. *Indigo blue. How do I make "indigo blue" more elaborate? And what about those readers who are not familiar with the color? What else is indigo-colored? What metaphor can I create? "The night sky." Trying to connect the sky to travel, I come up with "The night sky through which I fly." I like it—a little internal rhyme, "sky" and "fly"—within a free-verse poem. Starts it off with some rhythm.*

I consider what the physical parts of the passport—pages of stamps, size, number of pages—may represent, thinking like a poet.

Next I brainstorm everywhere my passport, or different versions of my passport, have taken me: Scotland and the cities I visited and where I studied, Italy (Sicily and Sardinia among other places), Paris, Seville, Budapest, Vienna, Gibraltar, London. I have been to many other places, but these are enough to be representative without losing the focus on the passport and travel.

I write "distant lands" but then reflect that it is not just the lands themselves but the "worlds" they contain, the cultures— food, language, dress, history . . .

I also contemplate what the different countries may symbolize and what I have learned from traveling. And I reflect on what this passport, what this traveling has done for me to make me the person I am today.

Since I am writing an ode, I need to celebrate or glorify my passport and praise it:

- *Evidence, Proof, Testimony, Confirmation of my travels*
- *Because of you, I have grown, expanded my own boundaries.*
- *With you at my side, I am confident,*
- *My passport, you are my guide*
- *Only you have made this journey possible*

I use poetic license to capitalize some of the nouns, drawing attention to them—Evidence, Proof, Testimony, Confirmation, Exploration, Discovery, Lives, Tolerance, Understanding, Acceptance—and turn other words into titles: a Citizen of the World, a Seeker of the Unique.

Because this is a free-verse ode (rather than a rhyming poem), the author pays special attention to line breaks, playing with placement to achieve the visual effect wanted. And then stanzas are redistributed so that the poem flows, has an organizational plan, and makes more sense.

Of course, much of this work—adding, removing, moving, substituting—takes place during the revision process; it is effective to show students the various stages of a poem. At this point in the unit, students are rough drafting (revision crafting is covered in Chapter 13), but a teacher think-aloud illustrates the process, gives students a model to emulate and techniques and strategies to begin.

STUDENT SAMPLES

A few student samples are shared and these students point out the descriptive and celebratory characteristics in them.

With two examples, "Ode to My Ring" and "Ode to Baseball," teachers could divide the class and assign half the class to critique one and the other half to assess the other, noting what they notice, or they could provide student pairs with both sample poems and request that they compare and contrast the odes. We also return to our lists of Elements of a Good Memoir. We review elements that these poems contain, what authors might add upon further revision, and what elements might not be effective, or even appropriate, for this writing (e.g., dialect). This activity demonstrates that not all memoirs will contain all elements.

The more models and the more varied the models, the safer students feel to create their own ode. They appreciate that there is not a "Right Answer," and there is no one way to achieve a goal.

DRAFTING OBJECT MEMOIRS

The students now have time to brainstorm and draft an ode or another type of object memoir, poetry or prose. No one is *required* to write an ode, but they can be encouraged to try this new type of writing, risk-free. Reasons to introduce and attempt to write an ode are both to create the challenge of a new format and to further develop skills of description and tone, two primary considerations in writing in this format.

This piece will not be taken further than a rough draft at this point, or assessed in a rough draft format, but will be placed in students' writing portfolios for later consideration. Later in the unit when writers choose which memoir drafts to take through the writing process (see Chapters 11 and 12), some will chose their object memoir and continue them as odes while others who chose to publish an object memoir will reject this format in favor of another format, possibly poetry, possibly prose, conceivably inspired by the original ode draft.

A student example is a poem that began as an ode to sidewalk chalk but became "Sidewalk Chalk of a World," a poem that could just as easily fit into the "memoir about places" category (see Chapter 6) and was most likely influenced by place-memoir study. Other memoirs that changed format or genre are highlighted in Chapter 11.

Sidewalk Chalk of a World by Jenn Levy

Wincing, as the sun provides a heat that keeps us
Warm inside. The piece of chalk and the mark that
Follows traces around the little waists of our bodies.
Finally, the masterpiece is finished, and it is time
To decorate.

What the inside world of sidewalk chalk can bring you
Is like when you go to Disney World for
The first time. It brings drawings to life and makes them look
The way you want them to look. Like the bodies of ourselves,
They're drawn in the perspective of what we hoped
And dreamed was the way we looked. Any clothes that were favorites,
Or wished we had, were sketched onto the portrait.

Some of us had freckles that popped out in the sun,
But we drew ourselves without freckles. Me, I drew little
Suns on my face instead, for I liked to think freckles were gifts
From the sun. A special number that He had given to me.

It was you who always wanted a purple dress with rainbow
Flowers on it. No one deserved a purple dress with
Rainbow flowers on them more than you did. The pavement
Was always generous, letting us create what our minds dared

> To think, giving us the opportunity to have the desire to be anything
> We ever wanted.
>
> The original had blue eyes, but the asphalt had
> Pink. Only you could decide if you wanted to have orange
> Or green hair. The pavement blocked out all other opinions and
> Cherished our own.
>
> Sidewalk chalk could take us on the ride of adventure,
> Really testing whether we could handle the imagination:
> Blue hair and pink eyes, and suns for freckles, staring
> Into the glaring sun that forces us to wince and keeps us
> In touch with the world of sidewalk chalk.

No matter the memoir format, students brainstorm before they write. They list

1. the physical characteristics of their object;
2. ties to any places, people, times, or events;
3. the emotional meaning(s) or representations of the object; and
4. any small moment memories.

Then they look at their lists, think about their focus, possibly conduct some organization, decide on the format, and write their draft.

ESSAY MENTOR MEMOIR

Students have listened to a song, read two picture books, and read many poems and odes. The object memoir lessons end with a short prose memoir, such as one by Mary Pope Osborne from *When I Was Your Age: Original Stories about Growing Up* (Ehrlich, 1996). In "All-Ball." Osborne shares the importance of the possession she bought for herself when her father left for military duty in Korea. "It was the best bouncing ball I'd ever encountered. Barely did it touch the wooden floor before it sprang back into my hands."

"The ball felt friendly, spunky, and vibrant. It had such a positive and strong personality that I named it before we even got home: All-Ball" (p.17). When the ball is punctured and torn to pieces by a neighborhood dog, Osborne is devastated but ends the memoir with the reflection that ball bouncing was replaced by other friends and activities even though she "slept with a torn piece of All-Ball under my pillow" (p. 22) until her father returned home.

This memoir effectively and with humor illustrates that prized possessions don't need to have a monetary value or be the representation of a great achievement; they simply need to be memorable. The story also serves as a mentor for another format, the prose short story or essay-type writing with which some writers are more comfortable at this point.

READING LIKE WRITERS

This is an advantageous time to require that students note what possessions may be important to the memoirist they are reading in their book clubs or individually and to notice how the author writes about these items, adding these observations to their reading response charts. An example is the words from *Chinese Cinderella* "I was winning the medal every week . . . it was the only way to make Father take notice and be proud of me" (p. 15).

Table 5.1.

What the Author Wrote (About)	My Thoughts	What I Might Try in My Writing
Object: silver medal "I was winning the medal every week . . . it was the only way to make Father take notice and be proud of me." (p. 15)	The silver medal that the author, then known as Wu Mei, won when she was in kindergarten was very important to her, mainly because it was the first time that her father ever paid attention to her.	*I might write about my archery medals from my first summer at Camp Lynnwood. I was surprised that I was so good at a "sport," and my bunkmates were very proud of me. Since I wasn't skilled at "regular" sports, it was one way to fit in.*

The teacher can explain how it appears that the silver medal that the author, then known as Wu Mei, won when she was in kindergarten was very important to her, mainly because it was the first time that her father ever paid attention to her. If the class is ready to move to the three-column, triple-entry journal, a sample reading response chart based on the book can be shared (see Table 5.1).

• • •

CCSS ELA-LITERACY ANCHOR STANDARDS ADDRESSED IN CHAPTER 5

CCSS.ELA-Literacy. CCRA. Writing 2: Write informative/explanatory texts to examine and convey complex ideas and information clearly and accurately through the effective selection, organization, and analysis of content.

CCSS.ELA-Literacy. CCRA. Writing 3: Write narratives to develop real or imagined experiences or events using effective technique, well-chosen details and well-structured event sequences.

CCSS.ELA-Literacy. CCRA. Writing 4: Produce clear and coherent writing in which the development, organization, and style are appropriate to task, purpose, and audience.

CCSS.ELA-Literacy. CCRA. Writing 5: Develop and strengthen writing as needed by planning, revising, editing, rewriting, or trying a new approach.

CCSS.ELA-Literacy. CCRA. Writing 7: Conduct short as well as more sustained research projects based on focused questions, demonstrating understanding of the subject under investigation.

CCSS.ELA-Literacy. CCRA. Writing 9: Draw evidence from literary or informational texts to support analysis, reflection, and research.

CCSS.ELA-Literacy. CCRA. Writing 10: Write routinely over extended time frames (time for research, reflection, and revision) and shorter time frames (a single sitting or a day or two) for a range of tasks, purposes, and audiences.

CCSS.ELA-Literacy. CCRA. Reading 1: Read closely to determine what the text says explicitly and to make logical inferences from it; cite specific textual evidence when writing or speaking to support conclusions drawn from the text.

CCSS.ELA-Literacy. CCRA. Reading 2: Determine central ideas or themes of a text and analyze their development; summarize the key supporting details and ideas.

CCSS.ELA-Literacy. CCRA. Reading 4: Interpret words and phrases as they are used in a text, including determining technical, connotative, and figurative meanings, and analyze how specific word choices shape meaning or tone.

CCSS.ELA-Literacy. CCRA. Reading 9: Analyze how two or more texts address similar themes or topics in order to build knowledge or to compare the approaches the authors take.

CCSS.ELA-Literacy. CCRA. Speaking & Listening 1: Prepare for and participate effectively in a range of conversations and collaborations with diverse partners, building on others' ideas and expressing their own clearly and persuasively.

6

MEMOIRS OF PLACES

BEGINNING WITH A TEACHER MODEL REMINISCENCE

When I think of my childhood, two places stand out—our backyard, just one of the continuous line of backyards stretching all the way up and down Hawthorne Road, and my father's jewelry store—one of the family-owned downtown stores in the years before the mall and fast-food restaurants came to the outskirts of town.

My backyard was a space of peacefulness and family gatherings. Its grassy expanse was filled with flowers and bushes and trees, backed by a rose trellis. I would sit under the maple tree and read. I would smell the flowers, climb up and down the slate stairs on the small hill leading from the back yard to the side yard, and explore the woods behind the house. Adjacent to the house was a flagstone patio with two pennies in the cement, representing my sister and me, dated the years we were born. That patio was the scene of barbecues, birthday parties, gossip, and stargazing. Up and down the street, all the backyards were similar, and all summer long the kids in the neighborhood would play in one or another.

On the other hand, my father's store was located downtown on Main Street in our small town, next to the shoe store and the drug store, both owned by friends of my father. In fact, all the stores were owned by my father's friends; he was also a friend of our dentist, our doctor, our lawyer, and our optometrist. During the Christmas rush, my mother, sister, and I worked in the store, alongside Frank and Ruth and my father. Besides the stores, there were three movie theaters and a few restaurants, and every street corner had a crosswalk where you could cross directly or diagonally.

Not everyone has experienced this teacher's idyllic *Ozzie and Harriet* childhood, but everyone has a place that is special—either the setting of a significant event or events or refuge from those events. Sometimes the special place is home or near home, and sometimes it is the exotic locale of a vacation or trip. What makes a place special are the memories, the small moments that occur there.

PICTURE BOOK MENTOR TEXTS

An introductory read-aloud for place memoirs is *Nothing Ever Happens on 90th Street* by Roni Schotter (1999), even though it is not a memoir. This picture book relates the story of Eva, a girl who is told to "write about what you know." She sits on her stoop looking over her street, writing, "Nothing ever happens on 90th Street," and, as she watches and captures the small details going on around her, she finds a story.

This story inspires those students who think they have no place about which to write to consider those everyday events that occur in places that have become special, not for where they are, but for what occurs there. Nothing *ever* happened on the teacher's neighborhood street or downtown on Main Street, but when this teacher consolidates the stories of many small moments spent on that street into one memoir and writes about memories, a story unfolds.

As a model for brainstorming, the teacher draws a picture of a childhood place. In the picture are replicated all the special people and events, as though a camera moved through time; then freeze-framed it.

At this point, an alternate or additional mentor text can be shared with students, David Bouchard's picture book, a story told through poetry, *If You're not from the Prairie* . . . (1998), in which the author describes the place he grew up, the prairie of Saskatchewan. On the cover Mr. Bouchard wrote, "We from the prairie are what we are and who we are because of the cold, the wind, and the sun." And the teacher thinks aloud that many of us are products of places.

In the book, each page begins with a line "If you're not from the prairie, you don't know the . . . sun, wind, sky, flat, grass, our trees, cold," and follows a repetitious format. The teacher follows Bouchard's format and creates her own poetic reminiscence of her backyard.

TEACHER MODEL

The teacher in the opening scenario models a few "pages" of a place memoir based on that special backyard:

> If you're not from my backyard,
> You don't know my trees,
> You *can't* know my trees.
>
> Maples that have grown for years and years,
> Providing a refuge for my laughter and tears.
> Weeping willows that bend to protect from the sun
> Providing shelter to read when I was young.
>
> If you're not from my backyard,
> You *don't* know my trees,
>
> ———
>
> If you're not from my backyard,
> You don't know bright flowers,
> You *can't* know bright flowers.
>
> Forsythia, lilacs, a trellis with roses,
> Setting the stage for a young girl's "Suppose's . . ."
> Tiger Lilies, tulips, dahlias in orange, yellow, and green
> Bordering a yard where I played and I dreamed.
>
> If you're not from my backyard,
> You *don't* know bright flowers.
>
> ———
>
> If you're not from my backyard,
> You don't know childhood games,
> You *can't* know childhood games.
>
> Statues, Cops & Robbers, and all types of Tag,
> Hide 'n Seek and Capture the Flag.
> Drawing hopscotch on the patio with colored chalk
> And shooting marbles, never watching the clock.

> If you're not from my backyard,
> You *don't* know childhood games.

As students watch their teacher struggle through a draft, crossing out, revising, using a thesaurus, moving "Tag" to the end of the line because it is a simpler word to rhyme, and attempting to discover something that actually happened and also rhymes with "roses," they observe how an author works, and they gain confidence, appreciating that poems and writings do not fall effortlessly from others' fingertips.

Those who are interested in this stylistic device but consider themselves less poetic may experiment with this format in prose, alternating description with small vignettes, while others follow the story-building technique of *Nothing Ever Happens on 90th Street.*

PROSE ESSAY MENTOR TEXT

Places can have more importance in our lives than we think; a place can develop us into the people we become. Experiences that transpire in, or because of, a place can prepare us for the future. Sometimes it is complicated to divorce events or people from places.

In Kyoto Mori's short memoir "Learning to Swim," the author discloses the ways in which the experience of learning to swim in the Sea of Japan and a near drowning in that sea helped her later, at age twelve, survive her mother's suicide. "She had told me to let go of her when we were both drowning in the sea. She was asking me, again, to let her go . . . while I swam with all my strength back to the rocks." This story could be considered a crises memoir, but teachers can include it with this lesson because it focuses on a certain place as the author constructs the story of going to the sea with her extended family and not only swimming in the sea for the first time but actually learning how to swim. It is a story of family, Mori's relationship with her mother, achievement, building strength, and of the importance of place.

POETRY MENTOR TEXTS

Cynthia Rylant's memoir of living in a small town in Appalachia—Beaver, West Virginia—is captured through her poetry in *Waiting to Waltz: A Childhood* (2001). While some of these poems describe people (see Chapter 6) and others relate events and crises (see Chapter 8), still others are about places in Beaver, such as The Kool-Kup and Henry's Market. The collection compiles a portrait of Rylant's adopted town, beginning with the poem titled "Beaver" and offering a thoughtful, reflective conclusion with "The World" in which the author contemplates "Going out of Beaver to the world."

The teacher can remind students of the hardware store in "Wax Lips," a poem previously read (see Chapter 5). For these memoirs about place, students can read a few of the other *Waiting to Waltz* poems, such as "Beaver," "General Delivery," and "Henry's Market."

A mentor text that builds on the odes presented in Chapter 5 is *Neighborhood Odes* by Gary Soto (2005). In this collection of poetry, Soto builds an entire community by presenting the events ("Ode to Weddings"), objects ("Ode to the Sprinkler"), foods ("Ode to La Tortilla"), animals ("Ode to Mi Gato"), and people ("Ode to the Mayor") that define the neighborhood. These poems illustrate that a place is more than a location; it is a setting for everything that happens there.

A STUDENT SAMPLE

The variety of poems in *Waiting to Waltz* inspires student writers to set out in their own directions, writing about a place that has special meaning, maybe for the one memory that occurred there or perhaps for those that repeated themselves.

At The Corner of East Del Roy and 51st by Kyle Firth

Frolicking, the sun's rays shine
Down on him
Like a
Heavenly hand from
God.
The ice cream van moving,
Moving through town with its silly
Jack-in-the-box tune
Playing, over and over,
Resounding in his head
Like
The beat of a drum,
Burning its melody into the
Mind of one
Distant
Four year old,
Standing at the
Corner of the street,
Money in hand,
Waiting for the
Ice cream man
To stop and ask,
"What can I do for ya, little fella?"
And,
Frightened as all get-out,
The child raises a lone finger,
Pointing at the goodness that is the
Chipwich,
A treat so delicious the boy will never again
Have anything as good as this
One treat.
But it's too late.
The ice cream man
Has passed.
Rejected,
He turns away,
Shoulders slumped,
Head drooped, and
Steps up to go inside.
Until he hears the tune again,
And he knows that there's hope yet.

Or the student who wrote about a world created by her sidewalk chalk (see chapter 5).

ANOTHER FORMAT OPTION: PHOTOGRAPH MEMORIES

Place memoir provides a suitable topic to write from a photograph. Generally a photograph of people can just be, well, just a photograph of a group of people, but a photograph of a place was usually taken because of something that happened or was happening in that place.

Using an article "Onset, July 1963" (2002) as a mentor text, teachers can demonstrate how the author, Ken Goldstein, begins his memoir with a photograph. As he describes the setting, "the front yard of my grandparents' house in Onset, Cape Cod, Massachusetts," he drifts into memories of his grandfather, the Onset house, and other events that took place on the Cape. At the end of the memoir, he returns to "Onset, on Cape Cod, in Massachusetts, in July of 1963." This is a circular story, or in many students' experiences, an "If-You-Give-a-Mouse-a-Cookie" story.

TEACHER MODEL

A teacher demonstrates the process with a photograph that her husband took in Rome many years ago: *The picture shows my son and me in St. Peter's Square outside the Vatican in Rome. In the photograph we are standing on a circular marble plate in St. Peter's Square. He is telling us that Bernini planned the square so that when one stands on one of the two identical plates, the rows on the nearest colonnade line up.*

She lets her story wander to other trips to Rome, starting with their first visit when, to their dismay, it was St. Peter's Day and everything in the city was closed; a future trip when her daughter was not dressed properly to see the Vatican, and she traded clothes so she could tour; later trips when the author passed on the story of Bernini's marble plate and took photographs standing on the circle with friends and other family members and had become very comfortable with Rome and its back alleys and many historical stories. These thoughts lead her back to the photograph and the first time she learned to love Rome because her son was living there and served as her personal cultural guide to the city.

STUDENT SAMPLE

There's Nothing Like the City by Katy Ament

In one of the few photos I have of my dad, my brother and I stare blankly at the camera, wondering who in the world is taking our picture, wondering whether or not this stranger will run off with our camera, our pictures, our memories. *Who does this stranger think they are, contemplating running off with our camera?* Something in me knew that wouldn't happen, though, because Dad was with us, protecting our camera and us.

We are happy to be at the zoo, to see the primate house and the lovely patterns on the zebras and giraffes. I am wearing a Baby Bop shirt and my hair is in wild pigtails, styled by who else but my father. Joe is sporting one of our millions of zoo keys, and I am wondering if today, maybe just once, I'll be able to turn the key myself and hear what the box has to tell me about the polar bears.

We would go to the zoo a lot. Sometimes we even met our cousins, Julie and Nicky, there. Joe and I would always know if they'd be there, but my aunt always had to make it a surprise for her children. We'd round a corner in the Playhouse, and there they'd be—Julie, sitting, smiling, in a dinosaur egg; Nick, goofing around, pretending he's being eaten by the fake alligator. As soon as they'd see us, their eyes would bulge with excitement, and, even though we knew they would be there, our eyes would do the same. "Cousin! I missed you. YOU'RE MY BEST FRIEND!" could be heard from the two girls, while shouts of Power Rangers and Teenage Mutant Ninja Turtles sound effects would erupt from the throats of the two boys.

On future visits to the city, Dad would drag us to the Art Museum, taking us through every exhibit. "Dad, we've *already* seen the European art the *last* time we were here." With Joe and me whining like we were on the way to the dreaded dentist, my dad had to do something to keep the security guards from wondering whether or not we were his real children. He would say, "Find a picture with a dog in it." I'd exclaim, "Oh, there's one! HaHa—I got it before Joe did." That would go on for a while. Then we would giggle at the nude statues on our way outside. We would look at the roof of the Art Museum and see all the different shapes and figures up there. The best part was on the way out, though. Dad would drive the car across the front of the museum, right at the top of the four million steps. Looking down on all those runners and dog walkers and bikers was like being on the top of a mountain, looking down over the city. Our favorite part of going to the Art Museum was leaving it.

Usually when we went into the city, it was just the three of us—Dad, Joe, and me. Mom would be at work, but we would go visit her in her Center City office later in the day. She had a big office with big shelves holding lots of books and a big desk that sat in front of a big window. Often I would *try* to look down forty-three stories and spot the pedestrians on the sidewalk below, but I never achieved this goal for fear that my itty-bitty little forehead would somehow shatter the glass and I would come tumbling from the sky. But I always knew that, if it really did happen, my mom, my dad, or my brother would save me, so I would try again. And again and again.

But for now, in this photograph, I am safe in my stroller, next to my dad, along with my brother. Joe and I are confused, still unable to understand why this unknown photographer is taking our picture, but we know we are safe with dad, my hairstylist, my usual photographer, my best friend.

Students discuss the fact that the memoir is about a place—the city—that is special to Katy, but it is clear that the story is really about her relationship with her father (and even her brother). Being with her family is what made visits to the city so special.

Students share what they notice:

- word choice—verbs "sporting" and "drag"; the adjective "itty-bitty" and the repetition of "big" as her mother's office overwhelms her;
- font techniques: the dialogue in all caps, which suggest shouting; the thoughts in italics; and the word "try" in italics for emphasis;
- specific details: Baby Bop shirt, cousins' names, the specific sound effects and animals in the zoo; forty-three stories;
- use of dialogue;
- hyperbole: even the Philadelphia Art Museum doesn't have four million steps;
- purposeful fragment: "And again and again";
- humor: wild pigtails; and
- the circular ending: back to the scene in the photograph but with a reflection ". . . we are safe with dad, my hairstylist, my usual photographer, my best friend."

LIST-POEM FORMAT

Again for those students who need a more simple format, the teacher can share a place list-poem, "Knoxville, Tennessee" by Nikki Giovanni (1994).

To mirror this format, students survey their place drawings, family photographs, or any of their maps and charts to identify a formative place from their pasts and begin a list of people, events, and memories associated with that place, considering order, line breaks, and word choice.

STUDENT SAMPLE

John created a rhyming poem in a list-poem format about his room and the memories it contained, masquerading as junk.

My Room by John Mousoupetros

"Time to clean your room,"
My mother said to me.

"Or you shall meet your doom.
I'll give you to the count of three."

I stared all around me
At all of the piles.
From what I could see,
Junk went on for miles.

A great big television,
Some weights, a punching bag,
A little clay bee (made by me),
Candy, equipment for laser tag,

A couple of game codes,
Plastic guns with a sight,
Shoes by the loads,
An orange flashlight,

Knick-knacks and pillows,
Dirty clothes galore,
A small weeping willow plant
(Yes, there is still more),

Tons of toy cars and
Tangled bike locks,
Glow-in-the-dark stars,
A collection of rocks,

Skateboards and hats,
On-the-door basketball net,
A cool tee-ball bat,
Some monsters that I met,

A one-armed figurine,
A bottle filled with mold.
This had to get cleaned!
I must do what I was told.

Well, I left my room,
So everyone watch out,
For I didn't touch a broom.
Please, no one shout.

My mom yelled at me good,
But I never really did care.
Only I understood
The memories that were there.

Table 6.1.

How the Author Wrote About Place(s)	My Thoughts about the Writing and the Significance of the Place(s)	What I Might Try in My Writing
"Our room became my refuge. Coming home from school every afternoon, I was ever so glad to cross its threshold, close the door and spread out my books. Doing homework was the only way to cushion myself from the harrowing uncertainties all around." (p. 51)	The use of the words *refuge*, *threshold*, and *uncertainties*—especially in that order—showed the stark contrast of the author's world outside the room she shared with Aunt Baba and the rest of her world. The threshold was like a door into another world, blocking out the uncertain world. I found it interesting that there is no physical description, but the author relies only on emotional description. As a reader I get the impression it wasn't what was in the room but what wasn't.	Describing what a place means to me and how I feel when I am there instead of describing what is in a place and what it *looks* like. For example, my backyard was a retreat and gave me sense of peace and harmony. It wasn't a refuge—I wasn't escaping from anything—but it was calming, probably because it was so natural and spread out.

READING LIKE A WRITER

Students continue to read their memoirs and notice *what* authors write and *how* they write. At this point, readers are asked to note any places that appear to have special meaning for the author. It might be an observation that was not highlighted by the memoirist but evident to the reader or a place that the author has identified as special in one way or another.

The example, again from *Chinese Cinderella: The True Story of an Unwanted Daughter,* is based on the room Adeline shares with her Aunt Baba, a place of "refuge" to young Adeline. Yen Mah also writes about her schools and the influence of school, her school friends, and education on her life (see Table 6.1).

Students can use a chart similar to the triple-entry reflection chart included in Chapter 5.

• • •

CCSS ELA-LITERACY ANCHOR STANDARDS ADDRESSED IN CHAPTER 6

CCSS.ELA-Literacy. CCRA. Writing 2: Write informative/explanatory texts to examine and convey complex ideas and information clearly and accurately through the effective selection, organization, and analysis of content.

CCSS.ELA-Literacy. CCRA. Writing 3: Write narratives to develop real or imagined experiences or events using effective technique, well-chosen details and well-structured event sequences.

CCSS.ELA-Literacy. CCRA. Writing 4: Produce clear and coherent writing in which the development, organization, and style are appropriate to task, purpose, and audience.

CCSS.ELA-Literacy. CCRA. Writing 5: Develop and strengthen writing as needed by planning, revising, editing, rewriting, or trying a new approach.

CCSS.ELA-Literacy. CCRA. Writing 7: Conduct short as well as more sustained research projects based on focused questions, demonstrating understanding of the subject under investigation.

CCSS.ELA-Literacy. CCRA. Writing 9: Draw evidence from literary or informational texts to support analysis, reflection, and research.

CCSS.ELA-Literacy. CCRA. Writing 10: Write routinely over extended time frames (time for research, reflection, and revision) and shorter time frames (a single sitting or a day or two) for a range of tasks, purposes, and audiences.

CCSS.ELA-Literacy. CCRA. Reading 1: Read closely to determine what the text says explicitly and to make logical inferences from it; cite specific textual evidence when writing or speaking to support conclusions drawn from the text.

CCSS.ELA-Literacy. CCRA. Reading 2: Determine central ideas or themes of a text and analyze their development; summarize the key supporting details and ideas.

CCSS.ELA-Literacy. CCRA. Reading 4: Interpret words and phrases as they are used in a text, including determining technical, connotative, and figurative meanings, and analyze how specific word choices shape meaning or tone.

CCSS.ELA-Literacy. CCRA. Reading 6: Assess how point of view or purpose shapes the content and style of a text.

CCSS.ELA-Literacy. CCRA. Reading 9: Analyze how two or more texts address similar themes or topics in order to build knowledge or to compare the approaches the authors take.

MEMOIRS OF PEOPLE
AND RELATIONSHIPS

When those who win awards or medals, realize goals, or achieve success in their fields are interviewed, typically they recognize or mention the person or people who inspired, influenced, mentored, or supported them. John Donne (1839) wrote, "No man is an island." Relationships sustain and support us and, positive or negative, make us who we are.

Generally adolescents do not dwell on those who have been instrumental in their development, the relationships that sustained and fortified them. Children and teens, who may shift friendships weekly, at times take relationships for granted. It is advantageous that they stop and look back. As much as environments, mementoes, and events shape us, there are usually people or relationships somehow involved. As Mary Kate ruminated on her friendship with Sam (see Introduction) she focused on the relationship rather than the person.

Teachers can begin this section by referring back to *Sweet, Sweet Memory* (chapter 1) and Sarah's relationship with her Grandpa, even after his death, and to Gary Paulsen (chapter 2), who wrote about not only the books that transformed his life, but also the librarian who gave them to him.

An enjoyable and effective read-aloud memoir with which to begin talking about people and relationships is Cynthia Rylant's prose narrative *When the Relatives Came* (1985). Many students will be familiar with this story from earlier grades and reminisce as it is read aloud. In her picture book, Ms. Rylant describes the annual visit of her relatives: "They hugged us for hours." The reader never meets any of the individual relatives—they are essentially a collective—but readers certainly learn what they and their visits meant to the author and her family who found themselves "missing them" when they left. "And they missed us."

Relatives are very important to our students, in even our transient age, and grandparents hold as much importance now—or maybe *again*—as ever. According to Amy Goyer, "The number of children living in a grandparent's home has increased significantly over the past decade, according to new data from the U.S. Census Bureau." In her 2010 report for AARP, Ms. Goyer shares the statistic that "4.9 million children (7 percent) under age 18 live in grandparent-headed households." Many of our students who do not live in grandparent households are very close to their grandparents.

Grandparent Poems, compiled by John Micklos Jr. (2004), presents a collection of poems written by a variety of poets about their grandparents. The poems are appropriate mentor texts, presenting a variety of relationships in diverse poetic forms, some rhyming and some free-verse.

A prime example is the tribute "In Grandpa's House" in which Rebecca Kai Dotlich remembers her grandfather charting her "growth" on his wall, and also Crescent Dragonwagon's poem "Grandma Louise's Gingerbread" in which she recounts how she "kind of know[s]" a grandmother she never met through her gingerbread recipe. As the poems are read aloud, students jot down what they noticed and what they liked for the discussion that follows.

To present another genre, the lyrics of Reba McEntire's song, "The Greatest Man I Never Knew" can be distributed, and students follow them as they listen to the song. After a second reading, students discuss the lyrics and the meaning behind them, an example of probing complex text.

At this point, writers have been introduced to mentor texts in prose, poetry, and song. As one more genre, teachers can return to Bill Cosby (2005) and his oral storytelling of "Old Weird Harold" and "Fat Albert."

An alternative, or addition, is Sonya Sones's poignant *Stop Pretending: What Happened When My Big Sister Went Crazy*, a free-verse memoir that chronicles her thirteenth year and her shifting relationships with friends and a family bearing the strain of an older child having a mental breakdown. While the writing is actually a verse novel-memoir, poems from different times and situations of the year express a variability of moods and tones, and teachers can select a few poems to share, such as "My Sister's Christmas Eve Breakdown," "To the Rescue," "February 15th," and "Memorial Day." A similar book is Lee Bennett Hopkins's poignant collection *Been to Yesterdays: Poems of a Life* (1995), in which the poet chronicles his parents' divorce and the aftermath. Some proficient or advanced writers may wish to use these memoirs as exemplars to tackle writing a longer piece comprised of free-verse poems.

The class critiques the mentor texts—picture book, poetry, lyrics, speeches, and prose essays, such as "The Long Closet," Jane Yolen's poignant story of her relationship with each of her grandparents, or "Food From the Outside," Rita Williams-Garcia's hilarious story of her mother's cooking (Ehrlich, 2002)—and analyzes the relationships and how they are described through the various writings.

When students reflect on these mentor memoirs and those that they already read for other memoir writings, depending on which types of memoirs have been introduced in the unit thus far, they realize that

- memoirists as a group write about a variety of people—predominantly relatives and friends but also neighbors, shopkeepers, teachers, strangers whose paths they have crossed, and even adversaries and relationships;
- there are many types of relationships;
- relationships can change over time or through circumstances.

Students return to their Memories chart or hearts. As students look through their charts, they are asked to notice which small moments include other people. One student's small moment about baseball involved "my friend Nick caught the ball when the ball hit foul." Kyree's memory of the pool included "a race with my friend." While these memories may not focus on people, there are many times it is the people involved that make the memory special.

After students peruse their charts, they choose three or four people, consider the relationships, and try a few free writes. Fifth-grade student Shuhan wrote about a woman he never actually got to know but with whom he had a relationship that he still remembers.

> I remember when I was little there is a very nice lady who owned a store. Every time I adventured there she give me some snacks, drinks, and other goodies. I was very happy. The next time I dashed to the store and she was not there. I asked the worker, "Where is the lady?" The worker declared, "She sold the store." I was very depressed when I heard that, so I began to walk home and explained to my mom what happened. Every time I went to the store I remembered her.

One of Shuhan's takeaways from his free write was now that he reflects on the episode, he realizes that he "really didn't think about her and our relationship until she was gone."

To assist writers in thinking and writing more effectively about the special person or people in their lives, it may help to let them imagine this person as a character in a narrative of their lives. Adolescents are more practiced at looking for character relationships and motivations in literature than in life.

A character development chart helps writers bring the person alive for the reader and may facilitate the writer's own appreciation for just what makes the person so significant. Teachers should only use a chart for those students who cannot find their way into a "person" writing, not to stifle the more advanced writers who are focusing on the relationship rather than the person.

Character Development Chart

Gender:

Age:

Culture (ethnicity/religion/race/citizenship):

Physical Characteristics:

Family:

Most Important Beings/Things in His or Her Life:

Positive Relationships:

Negative Relationships:

Likes:

Dislikes/Phobias:

Personality/Temperament (multiple character traits):

Endearing Quality or Behavior:

Quirks of Behavior/Flaws:

Unusual Habit:

An Object Usually in Pocket/Purse/Backpack:

Favorite Saying or Word:

Worst Failure:

Greatest Success:

Greatest Fear:

Greatest Hope or Desire:

Motivation for Behaviors/Successes/Failures:

Teachers can add any topics that might support students, and writers can fill in only those topics that would aid or enhance their writing. A character analysis such as this may generate the memoir reflection as we sometimes need to think about *why* people act in the ways they do.

It is more sophisticated to get to the heart of a relationship—teens in particular are involved in very complex relationships—and this might be one instance where a variety of mentor texts written in the teenage voice and student models by other young writers could be more effective than a teacher model. A well-designed and well-executed student model is "Sam and Me," included in the Introduction. A humorous chronicle that could only have been written by a teen is Christine's memoir "Stupid Boy."

Stupid Boy by Christina McDonald

I never really believed
Boys had cooties.
Sometimes
I just said I did
So *that* boy
Didn't think

I had a crush on him
Or want to marry him
In first grade.
But
The same boy
Never liked you too
Because girls had cooties.

Like when he asked you
For your phone number
Just in case
He forgot his homework,
But so did the other 20 kids in your class.

Or when the same boy
Asked you
To be his partner
Because all his friends
Already had partners, but they ended up
Looking just as lost
As you were
And mad because
He picked a stupid girl
With cooties.

Or when that boy
Wanted to be
The messenger
With you
For the week
Because he thinks
It's the best job.

But finally,
When he doesn't believe
That you have cooties anymore
And wants your phone number
To call and talk
And wants to be your partner
because he likes you
And wants to be messenger with you
So he can be alone with you,
And that boy,
Stupid boy,
Finally has a crush on you
And wants to marry you

In the fifth grade,
But now
You don't feel the same.

But then
You're partnered up
For that stupid whale project
And all those feelings
About that stupid boy
Come rushing back to you,
And people tell you,
And him
You're going to be
Boyfriend and girlfriend
Even though
All these years were
Wasted
On that same boy,
Same stupid boy,
Who thought you had cooties,
And wanted to be your partner,
And messenger with you,
And have your phone number,
Still has all those things
Because everyone was right,
And that same stupid boy,
From the first grade,
Through fifth grade
Is still the boy
You called stupid
But only because
He thinks
He loves you more,
And everyone
Was right.

This poem chronicles a relationship that fluctuates over years and is especially interesting for students to note that Chrissy used the second person "you," rather than first person "me," to illustrate the universality of her experience.

READING LIKE A WRITER

Students are continuing to read their full-length memoirs, reading a whole-class memoir individually, reading in book clubs, or reading independent choices. At this point, it is appropriate for readers to analyze the people in their memoirists' lives and their relationships with those people. The first step is to think about the people who are introduced in the

Table 7.1.

Who the Author Wrote About	What I Am Thinking	What I Might Try in My Writing
The author writes about her Aunt Baba and their close relationship and as well as her father and stepmother who do not love her, abandon her, and tell her she is of no value	What I find interesting is that the young Adeline lets others' view of her alter her feelings about herself. In an essay about her aunt, the 7 year old wrote, "Though I am really nothing, she makes me feel special" (p. 52). Her stepmother, Niang, makes her feel the opposite "Standing beside her made me feel especially worthless . . ." (p. 187)	I might think about and portray *if* and *how* my relationship(s) with the person(s) I write about made me feel about myself. And I can think of how my father always made me feel that I could do and be anyone, and therefore, it was a real shock after graduating college when I went to an employment agency and they asked if I could type. I had so much confidence even when I failed the typing test that I convinced the agency to give me a job (<u>not</u> as a secretary).

memoirs. Are they "main characters" with whom the memoirists interact recurrently or are they "minor characters" who only appear in certain circumstances?

Students may want to keep a chart, looking for the more significant relationships. They also want to consider *why* and *how* the authors write about the people in their memoirs. They can add to their charts. Again, the example is based on the memoir *Chinese Cinderella: The True Story of an Unwanted Daughter* by Adeline Yen Mah (Mah, 1999).

• • •

CCSS ELA-LITERACY ANCHOR STANDARDS ADDRESSED IN CHAPTER 7

CCSS.ELA-Literacy. CCRA. Writing 2: Write informative/explanatory texts to examine and convey complex ideas and information clearly and accurately through the effective selection, organization, and analysis of content.

CCSS.ELA-Literacy. CCRA. Writing 3: Write narratives to develop real or imagined experiences or events using effective technique, well-chosen details and well-structured event sequences.

CCSS.ELA-Literacy. CCRA. Writing 4: Produce clear and coherent writing in which the development, organization, and style are appropriate to task, purpose, and audience.

CCSS.ELA-Literacy. CCRA. Writing 5: Develop and strengthen writing as needed by planning, revising, editing, rewriting, or trying a new approach.

CCSS.ELA-Literacy. CCRA. Writing 9: Draw evidence from literary or informational texts to support analysis, reflection, and research.

CCSS.ELA-Literacy. CCRA. Writing 10: Write routinely over extended time frames (time for research, reflection, and revision) and shorter time frames (a single sitting or a day or two) for a range of tasks, purposes, and audiences.

CCSS.ELA-Literacy. CCRA. Reading 1: Read closely to determine what the text says explicitly and to make logical inferences from it; cite specific textual evidence when writing or speaking to support conclusions drawn from the text.

CCSS.ELA-Literacy. CCRA. Reading 2: Determine central ideas or themes of a text and analyze their development; summarize the key supporting details and ideas.

CCSS.ELA-Literacy. CCRA. Reading 4: Interpret words and phrases as they are used in a text, including determining technical, connotative, and figurative meanings, and analyze how specific word choices shape meaning or tone.

CCSS.ELA-Literacy. CCRA. Reading 6: Assess how point of view or purpose shapes the content and style of a text.

CCSS.ELA-Literacy. CCRA. Reading 9: Analyze how two or more texts address similar themes or topics in order to build knowledge or to compare the approaches the authors take.

8

MEMOIRS OF CRISES OR DEFINING MOMENTS OR EVENTS

Adolescent lives are filled with daily dilemmas, choices, and emotional situations, at least according to them. However, it is important for adolescents to take time and consider defining moments in their childhoods—events and circumstances that have shaped the persons they have become and may influence their future roles.

"Crisis" derives from the Greek "decision" and the Latin "judgment" and can be defined as a *crucial stage or turning point in the course of something* or *a dramatic emotional or circumstantial upheaval in a person's life.* A crisis is not necessarily negative; a positive event can also determine a trend of future perspectives or actions and beliefs.

Therefore, for these writings, writers should be reflecting on incidents or events that changed how they think or feel or how they generally perceive the world.

MENTOR TEXTS

For younger adolescents, an appropriate introductory text is Judith Viorst's (1981) poem "Since Hannah Moved Away." While the poem may not be autobiographical, most children can relate to the aftermath of a close friend moving away. Ms. Viorst captures these emotions quite perceptively, the sky becoming "grouchy gray," the taste of ice cream turning bitter, and winter months seemingly lasting the entire year, in a poem that contains rhyme, alliteration, similes, hyperbole, and references to all five senses, illustrating that memoir writing, to be effective, contains the stylistic elements of any good writing.

"The Death of Santa Claus," a poem by Charles Webb (2000), succinctly captures the moment of learning the "terrible truth" about Santa Claus. Interesting also is the effect this moment has on, not only the eight-year-old child, but the mother who is called on to refute or verify his schoolmates' assertions. Written metaphorically, the poem serves as a clever and somewhat complex text for students to study. This poem also serves as a masterful mentor text for students to analyze those line-break decisions that must be made in designing a free-verse writing. This writing can be effectively paired with Norman Rockwell's painting *The Discovery* also known as *The Truth about Santa* (Rockwell, 1956), and students can compare the topic as presented through diverse media—written and visual texts.

An additional memoir poem—and "complex text"—about a crisis is "Trouble with Math in a One-Room Country School" by Jane Kenyon (2005). This poem clearly demonstrates the crisis as a defining moment; the poet ends her reflection with the student being brought back to the classroom "changed" in response to her teacher's punishment for asking a fellow student for help with math. Students can analyze the text to see how the author presented the event and how it escalated into a crisis that became a defining moment in the way she would view "authority" in the future.

These mentor texts are effective because they present small moments. Sometimes adolescents view crises as earth-shattering events, afraid that the "small" moments that they experience will not be viewed by others as "critical."

The Towers, landmarks
That were there so long,
Were now in pieces,
Along with those who are no longer here.

From that day forward, we
Were no longer the Big Guys.
We were the Victims
Of a horrible tragedy.

Marissa was one of the minority who write about world events; most, like Debbie (pseudonym), write about more personal crises.

The phone rings.
I am told to stay downstairs.
My dad is swearing.
Why?

My mom says there has been a tragedy
My cousin went to his ex-wife's house
And shot her.
Why?

I don't know what to say.
I hug my knees.
All I'm thinking is
Why?

Then I was at a creek
Trespassing, and there was a sign
"TRESPASSERS WILL BE SHOT."
Why?

I am taunted day and night
Trying to forget,
But I can't.
Why?

The class discusses the simplicity of the poetry, and someone points out that there is not much to say. What affects the writer is not the *how* but the *why*. The strength in the writing is the trespassing sign that we all have seen many times but now has added meaning: *Why would someone shoot a trespasser? Why do humans shoot other humans?* And the ambiguous ending: Is she taunted day and night by the "Why?" of *the* or *a* shooting, or does the final "Why?" question the inability to forget since the incident did not *directly* involve the author.

This student example models that a poem does not need to be lengthy or use elevated language to portray complex ideas, and it gives hope to struggling writers who see this type of writing as feasible for them. They are introduced to the idea of quality versus quantity.

However, a crisis does not necessarily need to be portrayed through poetry to reveal emotion. In "Abandoned," Emily discloses the scar left on her fifth-grade heart in a prose narrative.

Abandoned by Emily Primmer

In my heart. There's a crack in my heart that no doctor can repair. It will be forever broken. You scarred it . . .

The day you departed from my life, it shattered. I was lucky because my precious heart healed itself, but a crack remained, reminding me, every time it beats, about the day you left me to fend for myself . . . the day you left me crying and wondering why you would leave a helpless girl who needed you so much . . . a girl who needed you there as her friend.

I was so alone. You came, bringing love with you, but you left, putting the heavy weight of penetrating sadness on my shoulders.

The scar on my heart won't go away, no matter what. I've tried Band-Aids and stitches, but the memory still haunts me . . . that day, the day when you left the child who looked up to you and loved you so much, to figure out the unfamiliar world by herself in a time when she needed her cherished dog by her side the most.

Now, as a young woman, I understand what death is, but my poor heart continues to break even more every time I think of you. I love you, but you are still the first one who placed an unwanted scar on my heart.

As mentioned previously, not all crises need to be large moments or have a lasting negative impact. Many events give the impression of magnitude at the time experienced, but for us looking back, are more minor, if no less significant. Students can smile at Kyle's memoir "At the Corner of East Del Roy and 51st," (also included in chapter 6) but through their smiles at young Kyle, sympathize with the crisis of loss and the perpetual hope that is brought back by the ice cream truck tune.

At the Corner of East Del Roy and 51st

Frolicking, the sun's rays shine
Down on him
Like a
Heavenly hand from
God.
The ice cream van moving,
Moving through town with its silly
Jack-in-the-Box tune
Playing, over and over,
Resounding in his head
Like
The beat of a drum,
Burning its melody into the
Mind of one
Distant
Little four-year-old,
Standing at the
Corner of the street,
Money in hand,
Waiting for the
Ice cream man
To stop and ask,

"What can I do for ya little fella?"
And,
Frightened as all get-out,
The child raises a lone finger,
Pointing at the goodness that is the
Chipwich,
A treat so delicious the boy will never again
Have anything again as good as this
One treat.
But it's too late.
The ice cream man
Has passed.
Rejected,
He turns away,
Shoulders slumped,
Head drooped, and
Steps up to go inside.
Until he hears the tune again,
And he knows that there's hope yet.

As writers capture and relive these moments, they contemplate the judgments and decisions that may have led to them and resulted from them, perhaps making this one of the most reflective of the memoir drafts.

More student memoir samples are included in Chapter 11. Chapter 11 describes choosing the memoirs to be taken to final publication, written in the most appropriate genre. Many students chose to share their crisis through a creative genre.

READING LIKE A WRITER

Again, as students read memoirs, they are each prompted to analyze the writer's craft. They can return to the triple-column response journal of the past chapters—especially for those teachers who have not implemented all the drafting chapters. Acknowledging that writers pick and choose what to include in a writing, students should reflect and respond to which crises their memoirists chose to include and how they wrote about these crises.

However, an alternate form for those teachers who have followed this book in order, incorporating all the memoir writings, might be a form that examines the crises, events leading to the crises, and the outcome and also encourages readers to notice and note words that the author used to reveal the emotions involved. The example shown (see Table 8.1) is based on the memoir *Chinese Cinderella: The True Story of an Unwanted Daughter* by Adeline Yen Mah (Mah, 1999).

• • •

CCSS ELA-LITERACY ANCHOR STANDARDS ADDRESSED IN CHAPTER 8

CCSS.ELA-Literacy. CCRA. Writing 2: Write informative/explanatory texts to examine and convey complex ideas and information clearly and accurately through the effective selection, organization, and analysis of content.

Table 8.1.

A Crisis the Author Wrote About	What Led to the Crisis	The Outcome or How the Crisis Affected the Author	Affective Words, Terms, or Phrases the Author Used
At age seven—the betrayal of Big Sister who is easily bribed into siding with Niang, the stepmother, against her own brothers and Little Sister (the author).	Adeline and her blood sister and brothers were treated poorly—forced to live on the top floor, were dressed in old-fashioned clothing and hairstyles, and given little food to eat. They decided to organize and approach their father. However Niang divided them by recruiting Big Sister, offering her a room on the "family floor."	1. Adeline realized that she no longer can count on any of her siblings and that she is alone in surviving. 2. This event results in her loss of trust in people and self respect ("I am nothing") because her father and siblings don't value her. 3. She grew even closer to her Aunt Baba and, therefore, was doubly devastated when she was taken away to an orphanage and did not receive letters from her aunt for years. 4. Conversely, it caused her to study hard and aim for perfect grades to try to win her father's approval, a move that in the end saves her. 5. Her writing about her aunt was rewarded, and she started writing, finding pleasure, and later recognition, in her writing.	defected; my refuge; loathed; despised; life sentence of subordination; painful; harrowing uncertainties; "I am really nothing;" Caution; submission; humility; "simply too painful;" Writing was pure pleasure"

CCSS.ELA-Literacy. CCRA. Writing 3: Write narratives to develop real or imagined experiences or events using effective technique, well-chosen details and well-structured event sequences.

CCSS.ELA-Literacy. CCRA. Writing 4: Produce clear and coherent writing in which the development, organization, and style are appropriate to task, purpose, and audience.

CCSS.ELA-Literacy. CCRA. Writing 5: Develop and strengthen writing as needed by planning, revising, editing, rewriting, or trying a new approach.

CCSS.ELA-Literacy. CCRA. Writing 9: Draw evidence from literary or informational texts to support analysis, reflection, and research.

CCSS.ELA-Literacy. CCRA. Writing 10: Write routinely over extended time frames (time for research, reflection, and revision) and shorter time frames (a single sitting or a day or two) for a range of tasks, purposes, and audiences.

CCSS.ELA-Literacy. CCRA. Reading 1: Read closely to determine what the text says explicitly and to make logical inferences from it; cite specific textual evidence when writing or speaking to support conclusions drawn from the text.

CCSS.ELA-Literacy. CCRA. Reading 2: Determine central ideas or themes of a text and analyze their development; summarize the key supporting details and ideas.

CCSS.ELA-Literacy. CCRA. Reading 4: Interpret words and phrases as they are used in a text, including determining technical, connotative, and figurative meanings, and analyze how specific word choices shape meaning or tone.

CCSS.ELA-Literacy. CCRA. Reading 6: Assess how point of view or purpose shapes the content and style of a text.

CCSS.ELA-Literacy. CCRA. Reading 9: Analyze how two or more texts address similar themes or topics in order to build knowledge or to compare the approaches the authors take.

9

MEMOIRS OF WHERE
WE ARE FROM

As teachers journey through this book, if they only have the time and resources to teach one memoir, a memoir about where students "are from" would be the one recommended. Examining where they come from helps young adolescents consider the influences that shaped the persons they have become. Examining where they are from lets them target their passions for opinion and argument, writing topics that matter and lead them to consider the influences that shaped the motivating forces of the people they study in history, science, math, and in the daily news.

Writing about "where they are from" incorporates all the other topics: mementoes, persons, places, ages, events, and crises and can comprise a compilation of influences of the past. We are the sum of all our experiences, and we come from all those experiences. As Sandra Cisneros (1992) writes in her story "Eleven," "When you're eleven, you're also ten, and nine, and eight, and seven, and six, and five, and four, and three, and two, and one."

Therefore, this chapter and writing can be paired with all the strategies and activities outlined in Chapters 1–3 and 10–13 for a memoir-writing experience and, in addition, can include any strategies employed in the specific types of memoirs being written in Chapters 4–9.

MENTOR TEXT

The most well-known and effective mentor text to begin this study is George Ella Lyon's iconic poem "Where I'm From" (1999).

> I am from clothespins,
> from Clorox and carbon-tetrachloride.
> I am from the dirt under the back porch.
> (Black, glistening,
> it tasted like beets.)
> I am from the forsythia bush
> the Dutch elm
> whose long-gone limbs I remember
> as if they were my own.
>
> I'm from fudge and eyeglasses,
> from Imogene and Alafair.
> I'm from the know-it-alls
> and the pass-it-ons,
> from Perk up! and Pipe down!

I'm from He restoreth my soul
with a cottonball lamb
and ten verses I can say myself.

I'm from Artemus and Billie's Branch,
fried corn and strong coffee.
From the finger my grandfather lost
to the auger,
the eye my father shut to keep his sight.

Under my bed was a dress box
spilling old pictures,
a sift of lost faces
to drift beneath my dreams.
I am from those moments —
snapped before I budded —
leaf-fall from the family tree.

During a reading of the memoir, students note the multiple, diverse memories that build Ms. Lyon's poem. Teachers can introduce yet another way to recall and accrue childhood memories—a neighborhood map.

TEACHER MODEL

The teacher shows the students a map of her childhood neighborhood drawn from memory (and a little help from Google Earth) and on which has been labeled the houses of the neighbors she remembers. She draws an "X" at each spot where there is a story.

She tells a thirty-second story synopsis about each X'ed spot in the neighborhood:

- *The woods behind my house where I built a fort out of bricks left by our builder;*
- *Kathy's third-floor room where we designed and created paper doll clothes out of wrapping paper samples and her back-yard where all the neighborhood kids played "King on the Mountain," "Statues," and "Tag," among other outside games;*
- *college students Kitty and Sally who "let" me wash their kitchen floor because I thought it was fun and asked to do so;*
- *the Judge's wife, who every time it rained brought our roaming dog home under an umbrella (in the days before leash laws);*
- *Aunt Rae who had a booth in her kitchen—a real one with vinyl seats and a Formica table—and how I visited her all the time just so I could sit in that booth, and the wall running along her driveway that I climbed and jumped off; Aunt Rae didn't mind even though she didn't have any children in her house;*
- *Mary Lou's aunt had an apartment on the top floor of their house and would let us come up once a year to watch The Wizard of Oz on television.*

The storytelling lasts about five minutes, and the teacher invites students to add to their Memory charts any memories recalled by her stories.

The assignment is given: *Draw a map of your childhood neighborhood and mark an "X" at the spot of any story.*

Options are given for choice and also because some students do not live in times and neighborhoods where they play outside:

Alternative 1: *Draw a floor plan of your home and mark an "X" at the spot of any story.*

The teacher quickly draws a rough outline of her childhood one-story house and puts an "X" in her old bedroom. She relates the story of how her mother was so excited to finally carpet the bedroom (off-white shag) and how disappointed she was that she could no longer play "Pick-Up Sticks" and "Jacks" on the linoleum "parquet" floor. She put an "X" in the kitchen and reminisces about cooking her first batch of cookies.

Families are more transient now and many students are part of military families; therefore, another option can be provided.

Alternative 2 (if you moved frequently): *Draw a map of the state, country, or world and mark an "X" at the spot of any story.* One of the students drew a world map and put "X's" in Korea, Japan, California, and Savannah, Georgia. Another drew a map of the United States, marking "X's" where she and her stories have lived.

Students then sit in pairs and relate a few stories from their maps, jotting down any additional memories that surface during their partner's story-share.

Now that their memories are "warmed up" and writers have added another brainstorming technique to their toolboxes, the teacher references "Where I'm From" and asks students to look at Ms. Lyon's poem again and label some of the topics she wrote about and some literary/poetic devices she used. They are to note what they notice, such as smells of the washing ("Clorox") and her father's dry-cleaning business ("carbon-tetrachloride").

After they have had some time to label, either individually or in pairs, they share.

CLASS ANALYSIS SAMPLE

I am from clothespins, —*It's a free-verse poem*
from Clorox and carbon-tetrachloride. —*smells*
I am from the dirt under the back porch.
(Black, glistening, —*alliteration*
it tasted like beets.) —*tastes*
I am from the forsythia bush —*places—yard*
the Dutch elm —*proper nouns; specific details*
whose long-gone limbs I remember —*activities: tree climbing*
  —*tactile*

as if they were my own.

I'm from fudge and eyeglasses, —*events*
from Imogene and Alafair. —*relatives—parents?*
I'm from the know-it-alls
and the pass-it-ons, —*hyphenated nouns*
from Perk up! and Pipe down! —*family sayings*
I'm from He restoreth my soul
with a cottonball lamb
and ten verses I can say myself. —*religion*

I'm from Artemus and Billie's Branch, —*places*
fried corn and strong coffee. —*foods*
From the finger my grandfather lost
to the auger,

the eye my father shut to keep his sight.   *—family stories*

Under my bed was a dress box
spilling old pictures,   *—mementoes*
a sift of lost faces
to drift beneath my dreams.
I am from those moments—
snapped before I budded—   *—reflection*
leaf-fall from the family tree.

Students share their notes, from which the class can make a list. As the next step, students are invited to return to their Memory charts and insert any memories their class list has brought to mind.

TEACHER MODEL

The teacher demonstrates adding to her original chart (see Chapter 1; see Table 9.1; see Appendix D, reproducibles 2 and 3).

Table 9.1.

	PEOPLE	
RELATIVES *Aunt Es* *Uncle Sam* *Cousin Betsy* *Aunt Rae*	**FRIENDS** *Kathy B* *Roslyn P* *Mary Lou* *Cindy*	**NEIGHBORS** *Judge's wife* *Kitty and Sally* *Jackie P.*
	LEISURE	
OUTSIDE GAMES *Tag(s)* *Statue* *King on the Mountain*	**TOYS** *Mr. Machine* *Barbie* *paper dolls*	**ACTIVITIES** *ice skating* *designing paper-doll clothes* *jumping off Aunt Rae's wall* *Pick-Up Sticks and Jacks*

TEACHER MODEL

After students add to their charts, the teacher should share her poem about where she is from, projecting it and pointing out those memories already shared in class. The teacher uses this as an opportunity to demonstrate how she created her own poem by reconstructing the techniques the class deconstructed in the George Ella Lyon's poem.

"Back in the 'Hood" (with thanks to George Ella Lyon)

I am from King-on-the-Mountain,
Hide & Seek, Statues, and Tag.
Splashing in puddles on rainy days and
Cowboys and Indians, Cops 'n Robbers.

I am from maples trees and weeping willows,
Rose bushes, Tiger Lilies, and Forsythia,
Playing in portable pools on sunny days and
Pennies in the patio cement, one for each child.

I am from the Beegleys and the Painters,
The Krols, the Wards, and the Weges,
Visiting neighbors' porches and kitchens and
Walkways and steps, even those that didn't house children.

I am from paper dolls and Mr. Machine,
Hula Hoops, Betsy-Wetsy, and Barbies,
Playing hopscotch on driveways and jacks on linoleum floors,
And penny candy that actually cost a penny.

I am from ballet lessons and piano lessons,
Brownies, 4-H Club, and the Country Club,
Building cabins among the May apples and Jack-in-the-Pulpits and
Shana, trotting behind me on all my quests.

I am from *Ozzie and Harriet* and *Donna Reed,*
Lassie, The Lone Ranger, and *I Love Lucy,*
Watching movies at the Route 19 Drive-in and
Strawberry pie from Big Boy's.

I am from a small town and tree-filled yards,
Family dinners, barbecuing, and birthday parties,
Storing memories to build big dreams –
Endless with possibilities.

After the poem is read, the teacher retraces the steps, thoughts, and decisions made during drafting, pointing out the memories already shared and discussing some of the things added, based on deconstruction of the Lyon poem. The teacher shares how other added memories, if any, were determined, showing the process of construction; it is important to show students how to put the pieces back together once a mentor text has been deconstructed.

Even though the teacher's model memoir might also be written in the form of a free-verse poem, this sample is much more structured and rhythmic than Ms. Lyon's poem. The second line of each stanza has three items while the majority of third and fourth lines together have two. The two poems reflect the different personalities, and while the idea of the poem was borrowed from George Ella Lyon (note the thanks), all authors' work should undeniably show their own voices.

STUDENT SAMPLE

Where I Am From by Janel Moore

I am from bar-b-que,
From corn-on-the-cob and mac-and-cheese.
I am from mowed grass and tall trees.
I am from the never-finished playground
That has no swing or benches
As if time stood still before my eyes.

I am from teachers and scientists,
From Mandela and Martin Luther King.
I'm from "Don't do drugs"
And "Stay in school."
From *Respect* and *Be tactful*.
I'm from "Thank you, Jesus"
From children's church
And the gospel songs
I've heard many time before.

I'm from word games and puzzles,
Road trips and airplane rides.
But also from drive-by shootings
And trying to stay alive.

In my room are boxes
Toppling over with old pictures—
A time when I lived
With no cares at all,
A time that I will never forget
And never want to erase.

The ensuing class discussion centers on comparing and contrasting Janel's version (Roessing, 2012) with the mentor text. Students may point out that Janel also includes food, her yard, family, family sayings, and religion, but the writer also portrays the disparities in the neighborhood: "the mowed grass and the never-finished playground" and "road trips and drive-by shootings." She ends her memoir with the identical, borrowed idea of a box of old pictures in her room, not to reflect on those who came before her, as did Lyon, but on a time when she lived "with no cares at all." The reader assumes that her photographs are of her own childhood, not those of her ancestors. Janel has used "Where I'm From" to facilitate her writing—to impart ideas and teach the format but guide her in writing her story in her own voice.

Teachers should note that those students who more closely imitate, or even copy from, the mentor text are those who more likely would not have written anything at all, because either they would not feel confident or believe they were "getting it right." Experience demonstrates that mentor texts do not stifle the creative and innovative students.

Teachers can also display another student poem, such as Lacey's, for contrast, as students should view as much variety as possible so that they don't feel there is a "right" way.

ANOTHER STUDENT SAMPLE

Another Leaf on the Tree by Lacey Field

I'm from the sweet smell of apples
Burning from a candle.
Home dinners that are cooked
In crockpots all day long.
Families who laugh
Until their bellies ache.

I'm from a family that cares deeply
But sometimes doesn't show it.

I'm from affectionate Italian ancestors
Gossiping in circles,
Witty Irish precursors
Who tell the funniest stories,
The warm sands of Florida
Where I truly feel at home.
I'm from little knowledge of my ancestors,
But I am still proud to descend from them.

I'm from the generous God
Listening to me every night.
The Bible with its stories
That seem to explain everything.
The sacrificial Jesus Christ
Who died for everyone.
I'm from a family that doesn't attend
Church every Sunday, but I still have Faith.

I'm from the northern winter weather
Causing me to shiver,
Boat rides in the Atlantic
That I truly dislike,
Family visits to New Jersey
That I could do without.
I'm from a family that tries,
And I appreciate every attempt.

I'm from my mother's amiable laugh
Forcing me to giggle,
My father's turbulent temper
Which is nothing to be proud of,
My mom-mom's love for lush items
Which gets me in loads of trouble.
I'm from traits of my family
That aren't flawless,
But I'm still proud to have them.

When students analyze Lacey's poem, they note that the language is more sophisticated, she uses more poetic devises (imagery, alliteration, personification), and her writing is more structured and rhythmic than either Lyon's or Janel's; it possesses a structure and rhythm different from the teacher's. The entire focus or theme is her family, which is portrayed in the title taken from a phrase in Lyon's last stanza, "leaf-fall from the family tree." Lacey has not duplicated "Where I'm From" but employed it as a catalyst for her own memoir.

MENTOR TEXT

To provide a good example of a prose mentor text, teachers can read Cynthia Rylant's picture book *When I Was Young in the Mountains*. As the book is read and the illustrations displayed, students jot down the topics Rylant includes:

- people: Grandfather, Grandmother, Mr. and Mrs. Crawford, Cousin Peter, and the church congregation;
- environment: coal mine, johnny-house, cow pasture, woods, swimming hole, cowbells, frogs, black snakes, stars, and bobwhites;
- foods: hot corn bread, pinto beans, fried okra, white butter, and cocoa;
- activities: swimming in the swimming hole, pumping water, the snake photograph, sitting on the porch swing, shelling beans, braiding hair, and sharpening pencils with a pocket knife;
- religion: Sunday church in the schoolhouse and baptisms in the swimming hole.

The teacher may guide them to note that the book also ends with a reflection from the author as an adult.

ALTERNATE MENTOR TEXT

A second picture book that works well as a supplement to or in place of *When I Was Young in the Mountains* is *Momma, Where Are You From* by Marie Bradby (2000). As does George Ella Lyon, the mother in the story begins her story with images of laundry: "washing loads of clothes in the wringer washer" and "peach baskets full of laundry to hang on the clothesline strung from tree to tree." She continues recounting scenes from her childhood: foods, the neighborhood environment, family members and neighbors, games, chores, and culture of the times—the Washington Senators and Duke Ellington. Many of her memories of the earlier times revolve around the peddlers—the Fishman, the Ragman, the Iceman, and she introduces her childhood observations and questions about racial inequality. Though not classified as a memoir, the author says, "I wrote *Momma, Where Are You From?* to tell my son about a time and place where I grew up" (http://www.soentpiet.com/mama.htm).

Marie Bradby employs numerous literary and poetic techniques, such as repetition, dialogue, hyphenated adjectives, and chronology—moving from Monday mornings to Friday evenings. Therefore, teachers may later return to *Momma, Where Are You From?* as one of our mentors for trait lessons—organization, voice, word choice, and sentence fluency—as students revise those writings they are taking to publication (see Chapter 12).

TEACHER MODEL

One teacher shared her bilingual, multicultural background with her students through a beginning rough draft that was a blend of free-verse and prose memoir.

Where Am I From? (inspired by Marie Bradby's Momma, Where Are You From?)

I'm from a place where the sidewalk runs through the neighborhood
and people greet you as you pass.

My sidewalk runs down through a park and right to my cousin's doorstep.

It's where we run and hide on the BIG branches of the Old Gum Tree,
where there is a canopy of shade,

I'm from a place where we jump on our bikes, ride to the Woolworths,
drink shakes at counter, and get ready to race with a *primo* in tow.

"I'll beat you home!" my cousin yells.
"Oh, no, you won't. Last one's a rotten egg!" I yell back.
"Deal!" and the race begins.

When we finally make it home, the arguments start. "You cheated," we yell back.
Then it's settled with a game of rocks, paper, and scissors.

I'm from a place where you can see the sun touch the water.
Where the sand in my toes feels like the stubs on *Papi's* face when he kisses my toes.

Sometimes there's rain in the morning, but the sun quickly dries it.
So we splash at the shore 'til the sun decides to rest.

I'm from a place where you feel the sweat drip from your brow,
but you can quickly cool off in the waters of the shore.

Where *los domingos* are spent *con los abuelos* eating *arroz con pollo, frijoles,* and *flan.*
There are games of dominoes and talking about the day that Castro will fall.

You ask, "Can I go there?"
"Yes," I say. "We can travel through my pictures that speak of the memories
that seem so long ago."

The reference to pictures may foreshadow publication as a picture book (see chapter 11). After looking over the teacher's draft and commenting on what they notice, the questions readers may have, and what she can expand in further drafts, students begin another free write, beginning with the phrase "Where I'm From" or the phrase "When I Was Young in. . ." They write for about eight minutes and then pair-share something from the free write.

Writers next prepare to draft a text about where they are from or when they were young, either in prose or poetry, reflecting on the mentor texts and teacher samples introduced. The preparation includes revisiting their various charts—Sensory, Topics (Chapter 1), Small Moments (Chapter 2), timelines (Chapter 5), maps (Chapter 9); and any other brainstorming devices employed in this unit to date, highlighting items they may wish to use to illustrate their past influences. They also review the classroom "What Makes a Good Memoir" chart (Chapter 2).

STUDENT SAMPLE

Noting the use of phrases in her native language in the teacher's "Where Am I From?" writing, Romeo also shares his heritage and his New York City childhood, so different from life in his present environment, South Carolina.

Where I'm From by Romeo Sepulveda

I am from the dialect of the city,
from "Yo!" and "Tight."
I am from boogie down Bronx,

obstreperous, electrifying.
I am from the lights and the cars,
    the skyscrapers and stadiums,
    towering and rambunctious.
I'm from Spanish food and shortness,
    From Lela and Tio.

I'm from "Dogs are mad; you're angry,"
    From "You better not ask for nothing,
    'cus you ain't getting it."
I'm from *Our Father* and *Hail Mary*.

I'm from 167th Street and Cromwell Avenue.
    From *pasteles* and *quenepas*.
I'm from the scars on my father's head;
    he fell off my grandmother's 7-story building,
    yet still in perfect condition.

I'm from tons of albums in my grandmother's closet.

I'm from New York City.

ANOTHER STUDENT SAMPLE

Kathy combined ideas derived from the mentors George Ella Lyon and Cynthia Rylant and wrote a "When I Was From" memoir in the format of a free-verse poem.

When I Was Young in Prospect Park by Kathy O'Donnell

When I was young in Prospect Park,
The kids traveled in packs
Playing tag or just exploring in the "jungle,"
Which was really just a bush-filled field.
My dad used to entertain us
By kicking my big purple ball over houses.

When I was young in Prospect Park,
My dad grew all different kinds of plants.
Cucumbers, tomatoes, peppers, and sunflowers.
We seemed to have the most garden space,
And the floral fragrance engulfed our home.
Every year, I got to pick a flower to plant.

When I was young in Prospect Park,
I was an only child,

My dad's car caught on fire,
And we had to get rat poisoning.
My pet fish, Fishey, died,
And so did my Granddad.

When I was young in Prospect Park,
And it snowed,
My mom used to bundle me up
And pull me around in a laundry basket
Because we didn't have a sled.
I never felt the chill of the air.

When I was young in Prospect Park,
I used to leave rice trails after dinner.
I learned to ride a bike
And to jump rope.
Once I even caught a butterfly,
But what had took all day to catch, died in my hands.

When I was young in Prospect Park,
I lived in an apartment complex until I was six.
My life there didn't revolve around school and drama.
I was in my own little, carefree world,
Among all those buildings that looked exactly the same,
And I wish I could go back to a place where life wasn't
So hard.

When Kathy's poem, or a writing like her poem, is used as a student sample, teachers can point out not only how much the reader learns about Kathy's family life but also the lessons one learns in childhood, such as "what had took [*sic*] all day to catch, died in my hands" and that because she was with her mom, she was content sledding without an actual sled and "never felt the chill of the air." Kathy shares more of the experiences of her childhood than objects and people. Readers are invited to view that "little, carefree world" and feel her comfort in the sameness of where she lived, contrary to the drama experienced now by the eighth-grade girl.

STUDENT SAMPLE

Doug depends on effective repetition in his poem "I AM FROM . . ." (Roessing, 2012).

I'm from the jungle
Where I found my first salamander.
I scratched my knee,
And the scar leaves tracks—
Digs in my mind,
And refuses to leave.
I'm from the jungle.

I'm from the fort
Where I hid from enemies,
Hid from the monsters.
Names scream off the walls
And tickle my ears,
Carves names in the mind.
I'm from the fort.

I'm from the cave
Where I play Hide and Go Seek.
Lines of clothes were my disguise,
"Stealth" they call me,
For I can't be seen by the naked eye,
Hiding routes in the web of my mind.
I'm from the cave.

I'm from the battlefield
Where I searched for the enemies
That I must capture.
But when it's my turn to run,
So much like lightning,
It burns my mind.
I'm from the battlefield.

I'm from the imagination.
Time has passed,
But memories remain,
For the imagination lingered
And struck my weary mind.
I remember most, but not all.
I'm from imagination

READING LIKE WRITERS

Students are continuing to read full-length memoirs either as a whole-class shared text, in book clubs, or individually (see Chapter 3). At this point readers are directed to consider and respond in their journals to the following prompts:

- From what childhood events, influences, experiences—people, places, things, traditions, stories, religion, environment—is the author "from"?
- What childhood events, influences, experiences—people, places, things, traditions, stories, religion, environment—helped shape the author?
- How did the writing cause you as the reader to arrive at this conclusion?
- What ideas for topics have you gained from the memoir
- What writing techniques have you gained from the memoir?

Table 9.2.

Where My Memoirist "Is From" List Influences and Experiences from Childhood	Why I Think These Are Important (from the writing)	Writing Ideas This Gives Me, Topics or Techniques

• • •

CCSS ELA-LITERACY ANCHOR STANDARDS ADDRESSED IN CHAPTER 9

CCSS.ELA-Literacy. CCRA. Writing 2: Write informative/explanatory texts to examine and convey complex ideas and information clearly and accurately through the effective selection, organization, and analysis of content.

CCSS.ELA-Literacy. CCRA. Writing 3: Write narratives to develop real or imagined experiences or events using effective technique, well-chosen details and well-structured event sequences.

CCSS.ELA-Literacy. CCRA. Writing 4: Produce clear and coherent writing in which the development, organization, and style are appropriate to task, purpose, and audience.

CCSS.ELA-Literacy. CCRA. Writing 5: Develop and strengthen writing as needed by planning, revising, editing, rewriting, or trying a new approach.

CCSS.ELA-Literacy. CCRA. Writing 10: Write routinely over extended time frames (time for research, reflection, and revision) and shorter time frames (a single sitting or a day or two) for a range of tasks, purposes, and audiences.

CCSS.ELA-Literacy. CCRA. Reading 1: Read closely to determine what the text says explicitly and to make logical inferences from it; cite specific textual evidence when writing or speaking to support conclusions drawn from the text.

CCSS.ELA-Literacy. CCRA. Reading 2: Determine central ideas or themes of a text and analyze their development; summarize the key supporting details and ideas.

CCSS.ELA-Literacy. CCRA. Reading 4: Interpret words and phrases as they are used in a text, including determining technical, connotative, and figurative meanings, and analyze how specific word choices shape meaning or tone.

CCSS.ELA-Literacy. CCRA. Reading 5: Analyze the structure of texts, including how specific sentences, paragraphs, and larger portions of the text (e.g., a section, chapter, scene, or stanza) relate to each other and the whole.

CCSS.ELA-Literacy. CCRA. Reading 6: Assess how point of view or purpose shapes the content and style of a text.

CCSS.ELA-Literacy. CCRA. Reading 7: Integrate and evaluate content presented in diverse media and formats, including visually and quantitatively, as well as in words.

CCSS.ELA-Literacy. CCRA. Reading 10: Analyze how two or more texts address similar themes or topics in order to build knowledge or to compare the approaches the authors take.

WRITING AND PUBLISHING

ANALYZING MEMOIR WRITING

Learning from Mentor Texts

They sit in small groups of four or five students, desks pushed together, sitting in a circle on the rug, or sitting in camp chairs at the back of the classroom. In one group, a student is reading aloud to the others as they jot on sticky notes and place them in their books. In other groups everyone is busy reading to themselves, also jotting on sticky notes, noting what they notice.

Each group is reading a different book, but each has a picture book, a variety of memoirs based on her childhood, written and illustrated by Patricia Polacco.

As students entered the classroom they sat in a group of desks. It really does not matter how the groups are organized; by the time teachers implement the memoir unit, hopefully they will have built a classroom community, and group composition no longer matters.

The teacher should display five or six picture book memoirs written by Patricia Polacco:

- *My Ol' Man*, about her father;
- *My Rotten Redheaded Older Brother*, about her brother;
- *Thundercake*, a story about her grandmother and a fear of thunder;
- *Some Birthday!*, about her father's plans for Patricia's birthday;
- *Betty Doll*, about her mother's special memento; and
- *Meteor*, about an event that involved the entire town.

Students will be familiar with Polacco's memoirs from the read-aloud of *The Keeping Quilt* (see Chapter 5). The books they will be reading for this activity are some of her shorter picture books. Polacco was chosen as the mentor author because she has written memoirs on a variety of topics and because she is an excellent writer, her books containing exemplars of all the traits of "good" writing. As an added bonus, Ms. Polacco illustrates her writings, and therefore teachers can employ visual literacy skills as readers analyze the illustrations—the ways in which they add to the memoir and the choices the author-illustrator made to convey the ideas in the story.

Teachers can give a short book talk and let each group choose a book. If groups have time, they can look at a second book also.

The directions are displayed:

1. In your group, together or independently, read the book you selected.
2. Mark on a sticky note anything that you notice or that attracts and holds your attention or appeals to you—in the writing or the illustrations.
3. Look for lines and words and drawings that give the story emotion and demonstrate reflection on the author's part.

4. Mark examples in your book from our class list of "Features of a Good Memoir" (see Chapter 2).
5. Mark any additional features we can add to the list.
6. What do you notice about the writing? Mark with your sticky notes any examples you see of good writing techniques. Name the technique or trait on your sticky note.
7. Discuss and compare your sticky notes in your group and make two lists:
    a. Any additional features to add to "Features of a Good Memoir";
    b. "Characteristics (Traits) of Good Writing."

As an alternative to sticky notes, teachers can provide a double-entry chart for their notations (see table 10.1).

Table 10.1.

What I Noticed in the Writing/Illustrations	Name the Technique or Note Why Technique Is Effective

A TEACHER MODEL

It is most effective to begin with a teacher model with sticky notes and discussion, using Patricia Polacco's *The Keeping Quilt*, which was read for the object memoirs, for the examples:

I notice that when the neighborhood ladies came to help with the quilt, in the illustration they are all dressed alike; all the older ladies are wearing babushkas, and it looks like the young girls are not wearing anything on their heads but their hair is long and pulled back. This makes me think that all the neighbors came from the same place, maybe "backhome Russia." The illustrations are telling a part of the story that the writing doesn't.

Looking at our Good Memoir Writing list, I notice dialect. This story contains a lot of dialect, such as "babushka" instead of scarf and "challah" instead of egg bread.

Or by chart (see Table 10.2).

After all groups have finished reading and marking their texts, a class discussion can take place, and groups point out effective techniques employed in their books. With a document projector, they can share words, phrases, and illustrations more effectively.

Table 10.2.

What I Noticed in the Writing/Illustrations	Name the Technique or Note Why Technique Is Effective
sepia tones—beige pages and brown writing	Looks old fashioned and author is writing about the past and ancestors
"the wedding huppa," "kulich"	Jargon or dialect (special words or expressions that are used by a particular profession or group)
"the quilt welcomed me"	personification

STUDENT SAMPLES

Some comments are made about the illustrations:

"There are colored drawings, but there are also real photographs in frames on the nightstand and other tables." (*Some Birthday!*) Other groups nod and add that Polacco also uses this technique in *Betty Doll* and in *My Rotten Redheaded Older Brother*.

"The pictures let you see when the story takes place because there is an old television and camera" (*Some Birthday!*) "and telephones" (*Meteor*).

"Because *Meteor* is about her whole town, in some of the pages the drawings of people surround the words in a complete circle."

"And in *Meteor* you can see the expressions on all the townspeople's faces."

"In *My Ol' Man*, you learn a lot about her dad that's not in the story by the drawings. In one picture he has little pieces of Kleenex on his face where he cut himself shaving, and she is helping him shave and pick out his tie. He seems kind of absent-minded."

The group who read *Betty Doll* discusses how Polacco drew the illustrations in black and white except for the doll, which is in color, and they point out that it is similar to the technique she used in *The Keeping Quilt* where the pictures and pages were in sepia, and only the quilt was in color.

As some groups present to the class, generally other groups will go back to their texts and thumb through their books, looking for similar and additional techniques, conducting an even more *close* reading of the text.

Readers point out that there is not a lot of description of the setting because of the illustrations through which the reader can see examples of small-town and farm life. They mention that if there were not illustrations, the author would need more description.

Groups discuss some of the features itemized on our "Good Memoir" list that are included in Polacco's writings:

- small moments:
  - the meteor that fell on the town (*Meteor*)
  - looking for the Monster of Clay Pit Bottoms (*Some Birthday!*)
  - the accident at the carnival *(My Rotten Redheaded Older Brother)*
  - making a thunder cake during a storm *(Thundercake)*

TEXTBOX 10.1

A Fifth Grade Class Conversation about Patricia Polacco's Picture-Book Memoirs

Amahri: "I noticed she used real photographs."

Tabitha: "She used real photographs even though the rest of the pictures were drawn."

Emily E: "She wrote about a personal experience . . . when her dad tricked her about her birthday. It reminded me of a time Dad tricked me about going on a vacation."

Tanner: "Her characters were funny, and she described them really well."

Malik: "You almost could say you knew them too."

Emily P: "I noticed that the memories seemed really important to her"

Miriam: "Her characters remind me of people I know."

Tynika: "And the things that happened were like things that happened to me."

Kyree: "She used humor, but it was not crazy humor."

- ○ different adventures with Betty Doll *(Betty Doll)*
- ○ her dad getting a job as a reporter *(My Ol' Man)*
- specific details
- descriptions
- humor
- dialogue
- dialect
- background information
- topics relate to the readers' common interests and experiences
- makes a point
- a variety of characters included in the stories—not just the author
- metaphors and similes
- obvious exaggeration—hyperbole
- onomatopoeia
- personification
- flashbacks
- reflective endings

The students add to the list:

- illustrations
- color
- pictures
- dialogue
- an introduction (*Thundercake, My Ol' Man, Betty Doll*)
- dedications to family members (at this point students are not only reading like writers, they are reading like authors):
  - ○ *Meteor*—"To my family—who actually lived this remarkable event."
  - ○ *My Rotten Redheaded Older Brother*—"To my brother Rich"
  - ○ *Thundercake*—"For my Babushka Carle"
  - ○ *My Ol' Man*—"In loving memory of . . . my ol' man"
  - ○ *Betty Doll*—"To the loving memory of my mother"

As the groups share out, students are asked to consider author's craft and construct a class list of "Characteristics of Good Writing." Many of the qualities overlap with the class Memoir list, but this is a list writers can use for all types and formats of writing for the remainder of the year.

A class list from a typical class included:

- a compelling lead
- a reflective, thought-provoking conclusion
- an organizational pattern
- specific details, such as proper nouns
- examples and elaboration
- active verbs
- imagery—sensory details
- vivid characters and settings
- figurative language

- ○ metaphor and simile
- ○ personification
- ○ hyperbole
- ○ oxymoron
- speech
  - ○ dialogue
  - ○ thoughts
  - ○ colloquialisms: dialect and slang
- sound devices
  - ○ onomatopoeia
  - ○ alliteration
- repetition
- a variety of sentence structures

Group members give examples of each characteristic from their Polacco books to support their claims.

During the next class, students examine short memoirs by other authors to compare techniques and ways in which they vary by author and by genre—poetry, song lyrics, essays, and graphics. An example shared was that although some memoirs by other authors, such as *Always Remember Me: How One Family Survived World War II* by Marisabina Russo (2005), contain photographs, few offer illustrations drawn by the memoirists themselves.

Looking back at some of the books read as mentor texts for their drafts, one student observed that in Rylant's picture book *When the Relatives Came,* the reader doesn't learn anything about the individual relatives, but in *My Ol' Man,* readers learn not only about Polacco's father, but also about her grandmother and brother.

Another student reminds the class that in *When I Was Young in the Country,* Rylant does share facts about her grandparents with whom she lived but little about the other community members; readers certainly acquired important information about Dolly Parton's mother in her *Coat of Many Colors,* at least in regard to her values and relationship with her daughter.

When students dig deeper and think more critically, they usually express opinions that Polacco develops characters, plot, and setting more in her memoirs than many others who write short memoirs. They then add "development" to our list of characteristics.

Students also can compare the themes or reflections in memoirs on the same topics written by the same and different authors—relatives, events, and artifacts.

As part of their independent reading, students will identify some of the characteristics on their list and compare how Polacco employs those characteristics in the picture books they read to how the authors they are independently reading do (see Table 10.3).

Now that the classes have identified the Traits of Good Writing and Effective Memoir Characteristics, there presents one more opportunity as a whole class to consider these techniques in professional memoir writing in yet another genre. An example from a newspaper is David Holahan's hilarious memory "When Lobsters Roam Free" (Holahan, 2006). The teacher first reads it aloud for students to listen to the sound of the writing.

I always felt uneasy driving back from the fish market with my grandmother while that heavy-duty foil-lined bag full of squiggling, doomed lobsters was at my feet. This was a little too close to the food chain for my suburban taste.

Back at the beach cottage, she would place the animated bag in the middle of the dining room table while she unloaded the other groceries. Each time I checked, the congregation had moved a little closer to the edge. I swear.

I was about 8 years old and had just arrived for my summer visit when my grandfather, watching me watch the bag, launched into the story that would define my relationship with crustaceans. The credibility of Mad Jack, as we sometimes called him,

Table 10.3.

Good Writing Trait	*My Ol' Man* Example	Example from the Memoir [title]:_____
compelling lead	"Our ol' man . . . was a flimflam man."	
specific detail	"A raggedy man in unmatched socks and a worn plaid suit."	
metaphor/simile	"He collected stories like kids collect baseball cards, or fine ladies collect special teacups."	
action verbs	"steamed out," "spin," "glided," "howled," "burst," "pleaded"	
dialect	"Boot-poor," "a good yarn," "Da" "cruiser"	
sentence variety	"We followed Dad into the woods until he brought us to Potter's Pond. Then he stopped and pointed. It was a rock. A great huge rock."	

was unassailable. Annie Oakley taught him to shoot. He had made the acquaintance of the legendary warrior Sitting Bull—and had a Lakota tomahawk to prove it. These historic encounters occurred at Buffalo Bill's Wild West Show, but still, when Jack spoke, we drank it in like vanilla Coke.

"Last week," he boomed from his reading chair, flush with mischief and smelling of noontime sherry, "Mum Mum left the bag on the table for a long, long time." He paused, lit his pipe, letting his remark sink in. Indeed, she forgot about the bag entirely, as she puttered around the pantry, he continued, exhaling a healthy puff of white smoke. With a big gathering due for supper, rather than buying many smallish lobsters, she had asked the fish man to cull the granddaddies from the holding tank.

"So these giants, with claws larger than mine," he said, dramatically holding high his meaty right mitt, "they were left to their own devices for a very, very long time." Not only did they topple the bag over; they lobstered their way free. Thence they began to disperse as if they had been planning this cottage invasion for months.

He explained that once a lobster gets a claw-hold on you the only way to get it off is to smash it with a hammer. If you have one handy. And that didn't always work.

Why hadn't he stopped them? I asked.
He smiled sympathetically and said, "I must have dozed off."
When did he wake up?
"At the very moment one was crawling over my foot, heading for the stairs to the second floor."
Where are they now? I demanded.
"Here and there," he said, nonchalantly drawing on his pipe.
"Where and there?" I nearly screamed at him.
"Well, I was getting dressed this morning and I opened my sock drawer. . . ."
"They were in your sock drawer?"
"There was only one."

"Did he grab you?"

"It was a female, I think."

"Did she grab you?"

"No, I closed the drawer."

"She's still in there?"

"As far as I know."

"Where are the others?"

"Mum Mum found one in the laundry."

"Did she catch it?"

"No, it got away."

"Aren't you worried?"

"Not terribly," he said. "They can only live out of water for another week or so."

"What do lobsters eat?"

"I understand that they are fond of the peanut butter and jelly. . . ."

I nearly fainted. Peanut butter and jelly was what kept me alive.

I rushed into the kitchen, checking the bag on the way—it had moved at least a foot—to do an inventory of the peanut butter and jelly stock. From the living room, I heard Jack bellowing, "Be careful!"

The cautionary was unnecessary. I undertook the accounting at a snail's pace. Careful was my middle name for the next 10 days. It took me forever to get dressed in the morning, shorts and a T-shirt. It was the most careful summer of my life. I was careful even after my older brothers clued me in on the joke.

As they reread, teachers have students circle word choices that catch their attention:

- nouns, such as *congregation, mitt, invasion, cautionary, crustaceans, inventory*;
- proper nouns, such as Mad Jack, Annie Oakley, Sitting Bull, Mum Mum; and
- active verbs, such as *launched, boomed, cull, lobstered, disperse, topple.*

Next students can look for the qualities and techniques that they had identified as making memoir writing "good." They make lists and compare with partners:

- specific details, such as *sock drawer, foil-lined bag, vanilla Coke*
- oxymoron—*a healthy puff of white smoke*
- purposeful fragments, such as *If you have one handy.*
- alliteration, such as *smiled sympathetically, meaty right mitt*
- similes—*We drank it [grandfather's story] like vanilla Coke.*
- hyperbole—*Peanut butter and jelly was what kept me alive.*
- repetition—*Careful was my middle name . . . It was the most careful summer of my life . . . I was careful even after . . .*
- lots of dialogue
- a reflective ending

Now that writers have examined the author's craft in memoir writing, they can next explore genres, or formats, to find those most appropriate or effective for their memoir(s) (Chapter 11). Writers will be prepared to delve into their drafts to consider craft traits, such as organization, voice, word choice, and sentence fluency, and specific characteristics associated with each to revise their writing(s), then edit for conventions, and take to publication stage (chapter 12).

• • •

CCSS ELA-LITERACY ANCHOR STANDARDS ADDRESSED IN CHAPTER 10

CCSS.ELA-Literacy. CCRA. Reading 1: Read closely to determine what the text says explicitly and to make logical inferences from it; cite specific textual evidence when writing or speaking to support conclusions drawn from the text.

CCSS.ELA-Literacy. CCRA. Reading 4: Interpret words and phrases as they are used in a text, including determining technical, connotative, and figurative meanings, and analyze how specific word choices shape meaning or tone.

CCSS.ELA-Literacy. CCRA. Reading 5: Analyze the structure of texts, including how specific sentences, paragraphs, and larger portions of the text (e.g., a section, chapter, scene, or stanza) relate to each other and the whole.

CCSS.ELA-Literacy. CCRA. Reading 6: Assess how point of view or purpose shapes the content and style of a text.

CCSS.ELA-Literacy. CCRA. Reading 7: Integrate and evaluate content presented in diverse media and formats, including visually and quantitatively, as well as in words.

CCSS.ELA-Literacy. CCRA. Reading 9: Analyze how two or more texts address similar themes or topics in order to build knowledge or to compare the approaches the authors take.

CCSS.ELA-Literacy. CCRA. Reading 10: Read and comprehend complex literary and informational texts independently and proficiently.

CCSS.ELA-Literacy. CCRA. Speaking & Listening 1: Prepare for and participate effectively in a range of conversations and collaborations with diverse partners, building on others' ideas and expressing their own clearly and persuasively.

CCSS.ELA-Literacy. CCRA. Language 5: Demonstrate understanding of figurative language, word relationships, and nuances in word meanings.

GENRE CHOICE
Making the Form Fit the Function

Students sit at their desks, their drafts spread out in front of them. They are now choosing which drafts they want to take to the final publication stage. These decisions may be based on the topic, the characteristics of the writing so far, or the format in which they have drafted.

In one fifth-grade class the students reflect on their drafts.

Andrew enjoyed writing about his uncle who is in the armed forces and now is overseas. Since he misses his uncle he feels a sense of closeness when he writes about their former fishing trips. LaVerne has shared her special doll with the class during Show 'n Tell. She is not sure about her ode but knows she wants to continue writing about the doll, given to her by her grandmother. Rueben likes the beginning of his "When I Was Young" poem. He thinks, with some time and help, he can make it one of his best writings. He says, "I never thought about *liking* a writing and wanting to make it better."

An eighth grade-class has written drafts for all six different types of memoirs: age, place, person, memento, crisis, and beginnings.

At this point in the unit, students in all classes have:

- conducted an intensive study of memoir;
- studied the importance of memories and of reflecting on those memories;
- examined and acquired a variety of strategies to gather memories and information, targeting the most significant memories;
- read, viewed, listened to, and analyzed a variety of texts: poems, essays, short stories, picture books, lyrics and songs, personal narratives and reflections;
- learned to read like writers, employing reading strategies, analyzing mentor texts, and mining texts for writing techniques;
- examined and employed a variety of drafting skills and strategies; and
- drafted a variety of memoirs—from one to all six types—the most effective number being three or more. Even those who have missed some classes have a few from which to choose.

Now students are surveying their drafts and considering the piece(s) they wish to take to final draft and publishing stage. If time is short and writers have only drafted three memoir types, generally they will choose one to take to the final writing stages; if the unit is more comprehensive and students have drafted five or all six memoirs, they may choose two or three to try as a multi-genre memoir portfolio or presentation. Some students think of complementary writings. Others look for contrasting topics and types of writing.

In this writing phase, writers choose the genre in which they will publish. This is most effectively accomplished prior to the revision and editing stages because text may drastically change in accordance with the genre, and if writers have already revised and edited, they may be loathe to make changes, taking the safe or conventional way. This unit can present opportunities for writers to take risks and think "outside the box" without being penalized.

The Common Core College and Career Readiness Anchor State Standard for Writing 5 advocates that students "develop and strengthen writing as needed by . . . trying a new approach," while, beginning in seventh grade, writers should be "focusing on how well purpose and audience have been addressed" in English/Language Arts *and* in History/Social Studies, Science, and Technical Subjects. The Note on Range and Content in Student Writing states, "they begin to adapt the form and content of their writing to accomplish a particular task and purpose."

One strategy for addressing task, purpose, and audience is to teach students to write in a variety of genres, also referred to as "forms" or "types" in the Common Core documents. The majority of students may not be familiar with the vast range of genres and subgenres available to them as writers. The Range of Text Types to which students in grades 6–12 are to apply the Reading Standards include the "subgenres" of graphic novels, plays, narrative poems, lyrical poems, free-verse poems, sonnets, odes, ballads, epics, journalism, speeches, essays, and memoirs. The English/Language Arts standards in Range of Writing are less specific, referring to Appendix A, which states "students produce narratives that take the form of . . . memoirs." However, when students are writing, they are reading; therefore, writing in an array of genres leads to reading in an array of genres—their own work and the texts they use as mentors.

One of the most important considerations is to make "the form fit the function," rather than forcing the function to fit the form. If writers want to reach a particular audience, write for a specific purpose, or fulfill an explicit task, they need to be familiar with a range of genres and then anticipate which genre would best realize the function of the writing.

Teachers who have based their lessons on the chapters in this book have already introduced a range of formats: essays, short stories, picture books, song lyrics, speeches, stand-up comedy routines, illustrations, full-length memoirs, narrative poetry, rhyming poems, free-verse poems, odes, circular stories, and newspaper feature articles. Writers can speculate the reasons the authors chose the genres in which they wrote and then analyze the effectiveness of the form for the function. For example, in many cases a rhyming poem feels emotionally lighter than free verse because it lends a musicality to the poem. However, sometimes rhyme is used to carry through the story plot and aid memory in the retelling, specifically in ballads.

One very effective example of "form fitting function" that illustrates a shift in genre to effect a change in purpose or audience reading is an excerpt from Luis Rodriguez's memoir *Always Running* (Rodriguez, 1993). In the particular vignette (p. 24–25), Rodriquez recounts an incident when he and his brother cross the railroad tracks into South Gate, "an Anglo neighborhood." The two Chicano boys are attacked by five teenagers. Pushed and then held by one of the teens, Rodriguez looks on as his older brother is beaten. The author reflects on his brother's "pathetic plea from the pavement" to not tell anyone that he had cried, an attempt to hold on to his reputation.

Rodriquez changes formats and, in doing so, alters his focus when he writes the incident as a free-verse poem, "Race Politics" (Rodriguez, 1994). It is beneficial for students to compare and contrast the two versions of the incident to analyze what Rodriguez changed by altering the genre or to conjecture whether the format may have been altered to accommodate the change in perspective. Students can highlight words and phrases that are identical and then concentrate on what has been changed and ascribe that to the transformation in form or in theme.

Developing writers should be encouraged to try divergent formats for their writings and not be penalized if the writing did not succeed as well or effortlessly as a "safe" format might have. Writers may also want to attempt a memory in two genres to observe the end results. Many times writers find out what they are thinking as they write. As William Zinsser wrote, "Writers must . . . constantly ask: what I am trying to say? Surprisingly often they don't know" (Zinsser, 2006, p. 12).

Some less conventional formats attempted by students are shared in the remainder of the chapter.

FORMAT: THE SONNET

The English sonnet, a short lyric poem ("little song"), traditionally had a strict poetic form:

- 14 lines divided in three quatrains and a couplet;
- a rhyme scheme of ABAB / CDCD / EFEF / GG;

- rhythm scheme: written in iambic pentameter;
- the first stanza establishes the subject;
- the second stanza develops the theme;
- the third stanza finishes the story or idea; and
- the final couplet provides the conclusion or, in the case of memoir, the reflection.

If the class has previously studied sonnets, this would be an opportune time to apply that knowledge to a modern situation. If the class is not familiar with this poetic form, teachers could introduce the structure, and students would have some background knowledge of the form in a future study of Shakespeare. Alternately, students independently employing a writing resource (see Appendix C), such as *R is for Rhyme: A Poetry Alphabet* (Young, 2010), might discover a novel—at least in their experience—poetic form and elect to apply it to their own writings.

STUDENT SAMPLE

PJ decided to employ the sonnet form to narrate the story of his first swim meet. However, new to the form, after drafting he realized that he had not followed the prescribed English sonnet rhyme and rhythm scheme. Since he was pleased with his writing and had been consistent with iambic tetrameter and an AABB/CCDD/EEFF/GG rhyme scheme, he named this innovative sonnet format after himself. This is an effective way to show other students that if they know the rules, they can break the rules, as long as they are doing so purposefully and consistently within a writing.

There's a First Time for Everything, an Artesean Sonnet by PJ Artese

I hadn't been swimming for very long.
This choice I had made would not be wrong.
I went up to the blocks when I was told,
And I took my mark and hoped t'was not cold.

The gun went off with a very loud BOOM!
I then dove and took off with a fast zoom.
I pulled very hard and kicked just as quick.
With all of the leaders, I did then stick.

Halfway done the lap, I began to speed.
I saw that I had now taken the lead!
Trying so hard to not slow down and lose.
Every last bit of energy I used.

This 50 freestyle was now all done.
It was my first ever race and I had won!

Although there does not appear to be much reflection in his last two lines, in his "Story Behind the Story," PJ reflected both on the experience related in the poem and the way he related it and his use of sonnet:

This piece describes my first ever swim race. It was about five years ago. I don't really remember whether I won or not, and I'm fairly sure that I didn't. It was more the feeling of accomplishment. When I got out of the pool after those two short laps, I think I had a smile from ear to ear.

I love this title. It just came to me during the drafting process. I liked it most of all because it was its own reflection—my first win and my first ever race to begin with.

The reflection in this piece is there but quite subtle. It's the fact that even if I didn't win, swimming won me over and made me fall in love with it. It hooked me, and I have been doing it ever since.

FORMAT: THE LIMERICK BALLAD

A limerick is a short humorous poem of five lines with the rhyme scheme AABBA and a very jaunty rhythm that follows the rhyme scheme, roughly . . .

Line 1: la, LA, la, la, LA, la, la, LA (3 stressed beats)
Line 2: la, LA, la, la, LA, la, la, LA (3 stressed beats)
Line 3: la, LA, la, la, LA (2 stressed beats)
Line 4: la, LA, la, la, LA (2 stressed beats)
Line 5: la, LA, la, la, LA, la, la, LA (3 stressed beats)

STUDENT SAMPLE

Tyler planned to write a memoir about his family trip to Disneyland. He decided to use the limerick format for the purpose of his poem, which was to entertain and illustrate the situation, which he now finds comical to his audience, which he identified as other eighth graders, especially the boys. Since a limerick would be too short, he wrote in limerick stanzas. The limerick rhythm and rhyme (and reputation) made reading the poem as much fun as the trip.

Trip to Disney World, an Adventure in Limerick by Tyler Johnson

My dad packed the camper that morning.
Half of my family was still snoring.
I was in the shower;
We were leaving in half an hour.
I could hear the camper roaring.

Dad trudged in, waking every-one.
His voice was exploding like a gun.
"Pick it up," he said
As we rolled out of bed.
Our vacation to Disney had begun.

Finally, nothing but open road.
60 mph, the speedometer showed.
My sisters whining,
My brother crying,
I turned over and went into sleep mode.

We were halfway there when I awoke.
My dad, in front, cracked open a Coke.
The camper's engine starting,

My brother farting,
The silence I imagined had been broke.

Six hours more; I almost hurled.
My mother stressed; her hair curled.
The sun was beaming.
My sisters were screaming.
But why complain? We made it to Disney World.

FORMAT: OBITUARY

Newswriting is an advantageous genre to teach for informative writing as it is also an essential genre to teach for real-world informational reading. There are many types of news articles, and students should study the features of each. Many students have written memoirs in the formats of news articles, primarily as local news and feature or human-interest articles. This genre is most effective when combined with editorials or op-eds that relate the insightful portion of the memoir. Many newspaper columnists relate their own personal experiences in their columns, such as Lisa Scottoline in her "Chick Wit" column in the *Philadelphia Inquirer,* and some columns seem to be a running memoir, such as that of recently retired *USA Today* columnist Craig Wilson. These columns suggest another format for teen writers.

An obituary is one type of news article not typical in memoir writing. An obituary customarily gives notice of a person's death, although obituaries that focus more on decedents' lives, rather than their deaths, are more compelling and effective and more significantly honor the decedent. Although obituaries come in many forms and sizes, the standard format can be summarized to provide a template, still allowing, within that template, writers to become as creative as possible.

HEADLINE Announcement: Name, age, profession

Paragraph 1: Announcement

Full Name; possibly nickname

- Age
- Residence
- Profession
- Date and Place of Death
- Sometimes, Cause of Death

Paragraph 2: Short Biographical Sketch

- Date and Place of Birth
- Places of residence
- Childhood
- Marriage(s)
- Education
- Employment

Paragraph 3: Memberships and Community Involvement

- Hobbies, Interests, Activities
- Charitable, religious, fraternal, political, and other affiliations

- Volunteer activities
- Achievements

Paragraph 4: Survivors
Paragraph 5: Service Arrangements

- Date and Time
- Place and Address
- Type of Service

Paragraph 6: Donations

- Flowers
- Contributions "in lieu of flowers"

STUDENT SAMPLE TO MENTOR TEXT

An obituary memoir would not be a common subgenre for a teacher to suggest; however, this was the proposal of a teen writer. Chelsea asked if she could write her crisis memoir about moving from her childhood house in the format of an obituary. Surprised, her teacher asked why. Chelsea said, "Because when we had to move from our house to an apartment, it seemed like a death had occurred." Having verified that the form was planned purposefully to fit the function, the teacher agreed to the proposal as long as the writing employed the proper obituary structure. What followed was a memoir that not only portrayed the feeling of losing one's home but also served as a mentor text for future student writings. Addresses have been changed.

Obituary for a House by Chelsea Palo

10 E. Belmont Road, 14 years of age, Family Residence, Ridley Park
   Constructed in 1990, 10 East Belmont Road, Ridley Park, PA, was a great home until vacated in January 2005.
   Entering the house, one always knew there was a feeling of love and comfort. This house housed several different family members throughout its years of being owned by the Family: Joe, Kathy, Matthew, Amanda, Danielle, and Chelsea. There were also the nieces, Deanna and Stephanie. Friends were always welcome to share the halls of this mighty three-story home.
   This house was member of the Belmont circle of houses filled with love, friendship, and memories, a member of the Ridley School District, and a place filled with Philadelphia Eagles, Phillies, and Flyers pride.
   10 E. Belmont is survived by the eleven neighboring houses owned by best friends.
   The "funeral services" will be held January 8, 2005, on East Belmont Road, off West Ridley Avenue. Goodbyes to the owners will be said on that date. Calling hours will be from 8:00am to 8:00pm.
   In lieu of flowers, housewarming gifts will be accepted at the fanily's new apartment at 91 West Avenue in Secane.

STUDENT SAMPLE

Based on viewing Chelsea's example, in a subsequent year and class, Anthony followed her model and wrote an obituary for the loss of his physical ability to play trumpet in the school band when he acquired braces on his teeth.

Obituary to a Trumpet by Anthony Margidi

Brass Playing, 6, Stress Reliever/Performer

Anthony's brass playing, age six, died March 24, 2009, at Karkenny and Hayes Orthodontics in Ridley Park, Pennsylvania, due to getting braces on Anthony's teeth.

Born in 2003, Anthony's brass playing quickly became not only a major part of Anthony's life, his brass playing became one of the loves in his life.

Anthony and his trumpet often performed at Lakeview Elementary and Ridley Middle School concerts. They also performed in Ridley's Jazz Band, which toured festivals throughout Delaware County. The duo won many awards, including best soloist and sectional honors.

Anthony's trumpet-playing is survived by his percussion talents and loyal supporters: mother Rita, father Tony, younger sister Francesca, and many friends.

Anthony's brass playing can be visited on Tuesday night the 12th of May from 5:30 to 6:30 p.m. in the Ridley Middle School Auditorium. The funeral will be held from 6:45 to 8:00 p.m. following visitation. Burial will be a swift one, taking place from 7:55 to 8:00 p.m. in the Middle School's band room.

In lieu of flowers, donations can be made to Anthony himself or mailed to Ridley Middle School, Ridley Park, PA 19078. Donations will go towards saving for a new percussion kit including drums, cymbals, sticks, hardware, and pedals.

FORMAT: GRAPHIC TEXT

A genre that is currently popular with teen readers is graphic texts—not only the classic comic-book type, but fictional graphic novels, such as Gene Luen Yang's *American Born Chinese* as well as adaptations of novels—for example, *Twilight, the Graphic Novel* by Stephanie Meyer and illustrated by Kim Young and *A Wrinkle in Time: The Graphic Novel*, adapted by Hope Larson. Growing in popularity are graphic nonfiction texts, such as *A.D. New Orleans After the Deluge* by Josh Neufield and *The Cartoon History of the United States* by Larry Gonick.

Bridging the gap between fiction and nonfiction are graphic creative nonfiction books; two popular examples are Sid Jacobson's *Anne Frank: The Anne Frank House Authorized Graphic Biography* and *Yummy: The Last Days of a Southside Shorty* by G. Neri. Of particular interest for this unit are graphic memoirs—the well-known books by Art Spiegelman: *Maus I: A Survivor's Tale—My Father Bleeds History* and *Maus II: A Survivor's Tale—And Here My Troubles Began* and the more recent memoir *Persepolis: The Story of a Childhood* by Marjane Satrapi, as well as others listed in Appendix B.

A novel idea is adolescent students presenting their memoirs in sequential art, accompanied by text. While this format can be employed for any type and tone of memoir, it lends itself especially to those crisis memoirs that appear serious at the time, but while significant, seem less critical upon reflection from the vantage point of teenage years (see figures 11.1, 11.2, 11.3, 11.4, and 11.5).

MENTOR TEXTS

Any of the graphic works listed above, specifically excerpts from *Persepolis* (Satrapi, 2004), can be used for analysis of the graphic genre. Students can analyze the text, the illustrations, and the interaction between the two.

When examining the graphic works, students learn to "read" visuals and consider effectiveness of

- style;
- use of color or black/white or gray tones;

So I get this message from the boss, and he tells me that I have to take care of some "business" for him, if you know what I mean.

I figure that I'll check the place out, see what's going on. When I arrive, I see a large man, and I don't mean that he was tall. He's got a furry rat above his lip, and he's packin' some serious heat.

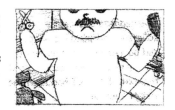

The big man tells me to cop a squat, or take a load off, if you will. He tells me that it'll only take a second, and that I won't feel a thing. Bologna.

He quickly goes to town on my frizzled follicles, with a SNIP! SNIP! here, a SNIP! SNIP! there, here a SNIP! there a SNIP! everywhere a SNIP! SNIP! You catch my drift.

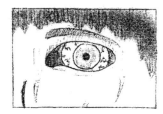

Figure 11.1.

As he REALLY started to hack at me, I realized that if I didn't act quickly, I wasn't gonna make it out alive. Thinking on my feet, er, butt, I let out a mighty battle cry, turning the tables on the big man.

Stunned into silence, my adversary dropped his weapons and backed up to the wall as I quickly made a mad dash toward the exit. I think I had seen the last of that guy.

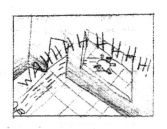

Looking back, I probably should've let the man finish his job, because for what seemed like forever afterwards, I took a lot of heat from my fellow men. He had only finished half...

Figure 11.2.

- image detail;
- size and layout of panels, shape of panel frames, and gutters;
- captions, narrative, speech balloons, and thought bubbles;
- lettering;
- sound effects and motion lines and emanate or symbols;
- "camera" angles; and
- anything else that captures their interest.

Writers also evaluate the text for writing strategies and techniques, as they have done in the other genres.

One appropriate short graphic mentor text is "Eye Ball" (Spiegelman, 2008), a nine-panel text by Art Spiegelman. In this graphic memoir, Spiegelman writes about one of the influences, amblyopia, that led him to becoming a cartoonist. Many teens are familiar with Spiegelman's *Maus,* and it piques their interest to read the reason he became a cartoonist (rather than a baseball player) and possibly compare these listed graphic techniques with those in *Maus.*

Another effective short graphic memoir, particularly when studied in contrast to the Spiegelman piece, is Derek Kirk Kim's "Hurdles" (2004). In this eight-panel memoir, Kim describes the hurdles that he faces daily, some literal as a member of the track team, and some metaphorical as the member of an ethnic minority. Indeed, Kim begins *and* ends his narrative with the line "I jump hurdles every day."

In this comic, essentially all text is narrated in first person on the side of the panel; there are only three panels that contain word balloons. The most interesting characteristic is the angles of the black and white drawings that give the impression of a camera zooming in and out. All the reader ever sees of the coach "Pear-Nose" is a close-up of his cap brim, sunglasses-covered eyes, and his pear-shaped nose as we "hear" his narrow-minded comments.

This graphic narrative gives readers and writers plenty to discuss in the drawing, the writing, and the message and serves as a mentor text to ways in which a short text can portray a larger meaning as the words and visuals complement each other. "Hurdles" also provided the model that Kyle imitated in his crisis memoir "Snip-Snip."

BEASTIE

By Kevin Andrew Shirley

I used to always want a dog.

But, I came from a family where the furry animals were despised.

Figure 11.3.

It made me feel
Out of place in a
Canine-crazy world.

The beast escaped its
Backyard prison, leaving
My mom, sister, and I in
Danger of being devoured.

I couldn't help but
Weep...

My heart was pounding as
The beast rushed toward
Us.

Until that one day.

Fortunately, its owner
Called it back in before
It could do any real
Damage.

Even so, I was scarred
Inside.

The neighbors were
Trying so hard to keep
Their beast in. They
Thought it wouldn't get
Out, but they were wrong.

Figure 11.4.

I never looked at dogs
The same way again.

Figure 11.5.

STUDENT SAMPLE

Kyle not only duplicated the formatting and drawing techniques of the text "Hurdles," but he also added his own touches to make the piece unique. The teen re-created the emotions experienced by his young self by narrating the scene in gangster or "mob" jargon, portraying the writing in the most appropriate genre. At a point, his teen identity realizes the absurdity of the situation and his childhood assessment of the situation, and in a stylistic maneuver he lapses into playfulness with a parody of "Old MacDonald Had a Farm"—"with a SNIP! SNIP! here, a SNIP! SNIP! there, here a SNIP! there a SNIP! everywhere a SNIP! SNIP!"

The writer also uses figurative language, alliteration, repetition, and purposeful fragments and establishes mood and pacing and incorporates many of the examples of good writing that students noticed in their Patricia Polacco book club evaluations (see Chapter 10). This piece features not only skillful and creative drawing but also effective writing.

Both the drawings and the text of "Beastie" were less meticulously rendered; however, Kevin incorporated elements of "camera" angles from "Hurdles," illustrating that, many times, only the most basic details need to be depicted to convey this poignant moment of crisis in a young child's life. While readers "see" the beast from young Kevin's viewpoint, we "hear about" the reality of the beast from its owner, a very effective technique.

As a student sample, Kevin's simple drawings and text encourage the more reluctant writers who may not appreciate the sophistication of both, but may actually achieve this level of complexity through the genre. Kevin himself might not have appreciated the sophistication of building tension with first a three-panel page, increasing the panels by one each page. Graphics also lets the artistic students not only shine in writing class but also more effectively communicate their stories in the same ways as picture books or illustrated essays.

There are innumerable genre options—brochures, A-B-C books, picture books, postcards, lyrics, raps, countless styles of poetry, one-act and three-act plays, and author-created genre blends, such as the haiku-ballad; students only need to look to the real world for examples. As an advanced option, writers create multi-genre projects that combine two or more genres. An example of a multi-genre memoir is Ruby Bridges's *Through My Eyes* (1999), in which the author supplements her narrative with pictures, quotations, and news articles. It is essential that students critically decide which "form fits their function," their topic, audience, and purpose.

Discovering the appropriate genre or mode of expression through which to tell their stories compels writers to pay attention in their readings to authors' decisions and enables writers to think critically about their writing in order to successfully convey their experiences in ways that make sense to them. Writing in multiple genres, and the choices that entails, makes writing both engaging and attainable for reluctant writers.

GENRES THAT INTEGRATE TECHNOLOGY

The Common Core State Standards require the integration of technology into the writing process. Many students are skilled with technologies and the use of such tools motivates and engages them in the writing process. Writers can further develop creativity and critical thinking skills by publishing a memoir through technology. In addition, allowing students to use technology tools in memoir writing means that students are allowed additional modes for making meaning, thus supporting student writers at all levels.

Teachers can use the storytelling format as a strategy to incorporate technology into their classrooms. Using digital storytelling platforms, such as iMovie, Photostory, or MovieMaker, are ways for students to create dynamic, multimedia memoirs that combine narration, music, captions, and both static and moving images. A digital storytelling platform that is finding increasing popularity is Scratch, a visual programming language developed for kids. Using Scratch, students can create a video game of events from their lives, a memoir that can be "played" like a video game. Another means of digital storytelling is through the genre of short film; students can write, plan, and record a short film using Flip video and editing in iMovie.

Those students who are interested in graphic art can enhance those memoirs by creating sequential art using technology tools such as ComicLife or ComicBook! These tools give students the option of drawing their own comics, or using photographs to tell their stories. The digital comic is easy to publish online for a real audience.

An effective way to integrate a number of modes into one project, creating powerful effects, is multimedia posters. Students can use a tool such as Glogster to create a multimedia poster that integrates texts, pictures, video, and sound. Since it is comprised of multiple modes, students can communicate in innovative ways.

Versatility in the writings in this unit gives writers a variety of skills and flexibility and resourcefulness that will be transferrable to other writings—narrative, informative, and argument—throughout the year, causing writing to become more meaningful.

• • •

CCSS ELA-LITERACY ANCHOR STANDARDS ADDRESSED IN CHAPTER 11

CCSS.ELA-Literacy. CCRA. Writing 4: Produce clear and coherent writing in which the development, organization, and style are appropriate to task, purpose, and audience.

CCSS.ELA-Literacy. CCRA. Writing 5: Develop and strengthen writing as needed by planning, revising, editing, rewriting, or trying a new approach.

CCSS.ELA-Literacy. CCRA. Writing 6: Use technology, including the Internet, to produce and publish writing and to interact and collaborate with others.

CCSS.ELA-Literacy. CCRA. Reading 5: Analyze the structure of texts, including how specific sentences, paragraphs, and larger portions of the text (e.g., a section, chapter, scene, or stanza) relate to each other and the whole.

CCSS.ELA-Literacy. CCRA. Reading 6: Assess how point of view or purpose shapes the content and style of a text.

CCSS.ELA-Literacy. CCRA. Reading 7: Integrate and evaluate content presented in diverse media and formats, including visually and quantitatively, as well as in words.

CCSS.ELA-Literacy. CCRA. Reading 10: Analyze how two or more texts address similar themes or topics in order to build knowledge or to compare the approaches the authors take.

TEACHING WRITING
Taking Rough Drafts to Publication

The student memoirists have chosen the draft or drafts they want to take to final publication and considered the genre in which they want each to be published (Chapter 11). In most cases teachers will have expected writers to design and redraft their writings in these selected formats. Some may deem this step to be a first revision since writers are adding, deleting, and moving material as they change the format, but it is best to refer to this stage as a new draft. Many students look upon revision as one of the ending stages.

Janel has decided to leave her "Where I'm From" poem (Chapter 10) as a free-verse poem but publish her place writing about summer camp (Chapter 6) as a series of postcards and her event memoir, "Standing in the Mirror" (Chapter 8), as a picture book. Chelsea will offer her crisis about moving (Chapter 8) as an obituary (see Chapter 10), her memoir about her relationship with her father (Chapter 7) in free-verse poetry, and her story about her first bike ride (Chapter 4) in a prose essay format, although today she might have converted it into the ideal digital story with a voice-over.

Emily, whose class has drafted three memoirs, chooses her origins poem to take to publication as "When I Was Young on the East Coast . . . ," the title and repetition borrowed from Cynthia Rylant's picture book (Rylant, 1993) but the format—free-verse poetry—taken from George Ella Lyon's "Where I'm From" (Lyon, 1999).

THE WRITING PROCESS

All the while, students have been taking their writing through beginning stages of the Writing Process. Some writings will go through a partial process and be filed away, possibly for more work or completion at a later time; others will be chosen to experience the entire process.

Many writers label the stages by different names, but the writing process essentially consists of

- gathering ideas or brainstorming;
- organizing those ideas;
- drafting—and redrafting;
- revising;
- editing; and
- publishing.

However, writers (and teachers) must remember that writing is not linear; composing, by its nature, is recursive. There are tales of classroom writings that proceed as Brainstorming on Monday, Organizing on Tuesday, Drafting on Wednesday, Revising on Thursday, and Editing and Publishing on Friday, teachers pointing to the Writing Process posters on the wall. This is not how authentic writers write.

Writers brainstorm, organize ideas, draft, and brainstorm some more, adding those ideas and details to the draft to develop and expand those ideas, sometimes reorganizing the draft into a different format. Writers then may be ready to revise, but that revision process may entail more brainstorming and drafting or even conducting some research to add support material and details. In between process stages, writers should discuss ideas and drafts, examine more mentor texts, meet in peer response groups, and if necessary, hold writer-teacher conferences.

However process stages are classified, what writers naturally do is

- begin with ideas;
- write those ideas down;
- make decisions about how to offer those ideas
    to their anticipated audiences (mode, genre, organization)
    for their predetermined purposes
- revise the writing multiple times;
- edit and proofread; and
- share with the public.

Of course, not all writing needs to be taken through the complete process to publication.

THE STEPS AND STRATEGIES OF TEACHING WRITING

The steps and strategies for *teaching* writing, as set out in this book, include

1. free writing for fluency;
2. brainstorming through a variety of techniques;
3. mentor text reading, analysis, and deconstruction;
4. teacher-modeling using;
   - reconstruction strategies based on the deconstruction of the mentor texts
   - think-alouds
5. considering student sample(s) of divergent types, lengths, and proficiencies;
6. sharing alternative mentor text(s) to allow for choice;
7. writing a first draft;
8. choosing an appropriate format or genre;
9. writing a second draft;
10. revision lessons and revising, for example;
    - Lesson #1—a lesson based on an organizational technique or skill
    - Lesson #2—a lesson based on a stylistic technique or skill
11. editing; and
12. publishing.

In their memoir writings thus far—whether they have drafted three types of memoirs or more (Chapters 4–9), students have experienced the first eight steps multiple times in divergent ways. They have used free writing as a strategy to activate ideas, and they have practiced a range of brainstorming techniques, using a variety of maps and organizers. Writers have been introduced to mentor texts in varied genres, such as poetry, essays, songs, picture books, novel-length memoirs, and speeches, written by a diversity of authors.

Students have also experienced *reading* like writers. Individually, and collaboratively with their classmates, they have deconstructed mentor texts—taking them apart and analyzing the components, characteristics, and techniques. Students then observed their teachers' thought processes as they synthesized their own memoirs, reconstructing those components and traits into new, unique, personal creations, thinking aloud as they fashioned their writings with the purpose of sharing their own methods with learners.

If teachers have taught this type of writing in previous years, they share student samples so that current students can survey writings that may more closely reflect their own. If this is a teacher's first classroom experience with memoir writing, they can share the samples provided in this book.

In all chapters, alternative mentor texts have been presented to allow for choice in writing. For example, if the primary mentor text is a poem, the alternative mentor text may be a prose narrative; if the central text is an ode, another choice may be a list-poem.

At this point in time, writers have drafted whatever number of memoirs their teachers have taught. They have chosen the one(s) they want to take to final publication and chosen the format (genre) most appropriate for their purpose(s) and audience(s)—or perhaps they have chosen a new or innovative format or structure as an opportunity to take a risk and try a new type of writing (Chapter 11). Some teachers may want to reverse the order of Chapters 11 and 12, but many find that if writers have revised, especially multiple times, they are hesitant to take the writing in a different direction from the original, now revised draft.

REVISION

Revision is the stage where teachers can *teach* the craft of writing and the characteristics of good writing. As Beverly Chin notes, "it is in this [revision] stage of the writing process that students grow as writers, readers, and thinkers."

Commonly, writing is characterized by six traits or descriptors when discussing and analyzing writing. The six traits of effective writing are those characteristics that make writing "work" and define good writing (Spandel, 2008). They are similar to the writing domains listed by some state assessments but expand the concept of Style, which includes voice, word choice, and sentence fluency, to three individual traits:

- Ideas
- Organization
- Voice
- Word Choice
- Sentence Fluency
- Conventions

Content, or ideas, is generated through free writing and brainstorming. Development of those ideas occurs as writers draft, discuss their drafts with peers and solicit questions from readers, and then brainstorm more to add supporting ideas and details and specific examples. Much of the organization of writings will be managed as each writer designs a comprehensive writing plan, grouping and sequencing ideas, using genre-specific strategies.

Many organizational ideas, such as leads, introduction, conclusions, and pacing can be taught during the revision stage and added through revision. Revision, in most cases, is appropriately the stage where stylistic devices, such as voice, word choices, and sentence variety and fluency, are taught and applied, together with any genre-appropriate strategies.

Above all, teachers want to avoid dampening writers' enthusiasm for their writings and should not expect finished writings to be "perfect." Sixth-grade writers should write like sixth graders; ninth graders should write like ninth graders. Very few students will write like published adult authors. Teachers need to recognize that their students are developing writers, and as long as writers are improving throughout the year and through the years, they are successful. The goal is to help students become *better* writers.

The Common Core State Standards serves as a guide to where students' skills should stand by the end of the grade to be successfully college and career ready. That does not mean that all students will progress to the same level. The hope is to keep the flame alive, so that evolving writers will want to write and want to write *better* and more meaningfully.

Therefore, teachers should not destroy interest in a piece of writing by demanding excessive revision. An expedient guide is to teach one element for each domain in each writing as students draft, revise multiple times, then edit. With many writings throughout the year, numerous writing lessons will be taught and implemented and reviewed: for example, a lesson on gathering or developing ideas, revision lessons on organization and one of the stylistic traits, and an editing lesson for conventions.

TEACHING REVISION THROUGH THE FOCUS LESSON

Focus lessons are ten-to-fifteen-minute lessons that are simple and direct, focusing on one procedure, element, technique, or skill, and are derived from the needs of the students. The most effective lessons are taught through the gradual-release-of-responsibility model. This is most effectively achieved within a writing workshop approach.

As the first step, the teacher makes a connection to previous learning—a past lesson, classroom conversation, or a mentor text that was shared—and gives writers a rationale for the technique—why it is useful to know and use. If the connection is not made to a previously read mentor text, a short mentor text can be introduced as a read-aloud.

Next the teacher gives direct instruction in the revision tactic by modeling the technique, thinking aloud while doing so. The students watch and listen. Sometimes this step is referred to as the "Teacher Model" or the "I Do" stage.

The students—individually, in pairs, or in small groups—practice the technique while the teacher watches and guides. This step is designated as "Guided Practice" or the "We Do" stage.

Last is the "Independent Application" or "You Do" stage where writers are invited to independently apply the strategy or technique to their own writings during the workshop phase of the writing class.

GRADUAL-RELEASE-OF-RESPONSIBILITY FOCUS LESSON EXAMPLE

Connection and Rationale: Teacher says something along the lines of: "You may remember that yesterday I asked Peter to get me a marker from the closet. Since I wasn't specific, he brought me a Sharpie, which I could not use because I wanted to write on the White Board. I should have asked Peter to bring me an **Expo**. Instead of a common noun (marker), I should have used a **proper noun—Expo**. A **proper noun** is the name of a specific person, place, or thing. In that way, Peter would have known exactly what type of marker to get.

Mentor Text Read-Aloud:

> The gym was in **North Philadelphia**, far from the glistening **Center City** business district. Going north on **Broad Street**, the white marble of **City Hall** was replaced by the red plastic of **Kentucky Fried Chicken**, the dark glass of vacant storefronts, and the fake wood paneling of check-cashing agencies with lines around the corner, like opening day of a first-run movie. Unemployment was higher in this area and the evidence was on every street corner, where the homeless shook **McDonald's** cups of change. (Scottoline, 2002)

The teacher points out how the reference to specific details by use of proper nouns ("Broad Street," "City Hall," "Kentucky Fried Chicken," "McDonald's") makes the scene come alive and lets the readers picture certain items and places.

Teacher Model (revision "Back in the 'Hood," Chapter 9): "I am going to revisit my draft of my poem 'Back in the 'Hood' (see chapter 9) to determine where I can substitute a common noun or add a **proper noun** to better show my readers my childhood. Let's look at one stanza as I revise."

I am from ^{Miss Sally's} ballet lessons and piano lessons,
   ~~Clubs at school~~ ^{Brownies, 4-H Club}, and ~~the~~ ^{Nemacolon Country Club,}
   Building cabins among the ~~wild flowers~~ ^{May Apples and Jack-in-the-Pulpits,}
   Shana, ^{a Wirehaired Dachshund,} trotting behind me on all my quests.

Guided Practice Activity: The teacher tells students, "In pairs describe our classroom, using as many proper nouns as possible. For expediency, you can make a list of proper nouns you could use in a description, seeing how many you can write down in three minutes."

Smart Board
Expo Dry-Erase Markers
Ticonderoga Pencils
Kleenex
Susie, Frank, Jake, LaVerne, Sarah, Courtney, Justin . . .
The Prentice-Hall Reader
The Merriam-Webster Dictionary
Thermos
Nikes

As a brief mentor text activity prior to the listing activity, pairs can pick out proper nouns from short mentor text examples and discuss the effect of the nouns on the reader. *Example:* "My eyes went over May's wildly colorful cabinets, and I was free again. I saw Oreos and Ruffles and big bags of Snickers" (Cynthia Rylant, *Missing May*, 2004).

Independent Application Instructions: The teacher invites writers to look back ("re-see") at their draft and note where they can change some common nouns to **proper nouns** or add some **proper nouns** so the reader can "see" what they are describing *more specifically.*

   Teachers can make a list of Organization and Style focus lessons, teaching one of each with each draft in this unit—and throughout the year. Some crafts and characteristics will better complement particular writings. For example, endings that are reflective conclusions, rather than summaries, are appropriate to teach during the memoir writing, and variety in sentence structure for pacing can be especially effective in a crisis memoir.

   Students will be revising each draft twice, but it is not necessary to rewrite the draft each time; writers can mark what they will add, remove, move, or substitute, filling the draft with carets, cross-outs, and arrows, possibly in a different color ink. If writers are drafting on a computer, they may want to use Track Changes before they make their final revision decisions.

   Depending on the number of drafts and the number chosen to take to final publication, teachers can teach anywhere from two to six revision lessons in this unit. Of course, the lessons do not preclude writers from implementing additional revisions, especially those based on past focus lessons, as they review and revise their drafts.

   The topics for many trait lessons can be amassed directly from the Common Core State Standards ELA-Literacy in Writing and Language themselves. For example,

Ideas: *CCSS.ELA-Literacy.L.5.8 Recall relevant information from experiences . . .*
Organization: *CCSS.ELA-Literacy.L.9–10.3e Provide a conclusion that follows from and reflects on what is experienced, observed, or resolved over the course of the narrative.*

Word Choice: *CCSS.ELA-Literacy.L.6.6 Acquire and use accurately grade-appropriate general academic and domain-specific words and phrases.*

Voice: *CCSS.ELA-Literacy.L.8.3a Use verbs in the active and passive voice and in the conditional and subjunctive mood to achieve particular effects (e.g., emphasizing the actor or the action; expressing uncertainty or describing a state contrary to fact).*

Conventions: *CCSS.ELA-Literacy.L.8.2a Use punctuation (comma, ellipsis, dash) to indicate a pause or break.*

Ideas, Organization, and Style: *CCSS.ELA-Literacy.L.7.3b Use narrative techniques, such as dialogue, pacing, and description, to develop experiences, events, and/or characters.*

FOCUS LESSON IDEAS

Lesson choices should be driven by classroom writers' needs; however, some appropriate focus lessons, depending on the grade level, are

Organization:

- attention-getting leads or "hooks"
- reflective conclusions
- sequencing
- transitional devices
- pacing (i.e., "Explode a Moment and Shrink a Century") (see Lane, 1992, Appendix C)

Voice:

- tone
- awareness of audience and purpose
- point of view
- dialogue
- choosing a topic for which the writer has understanding and commitment
- publishing in an appropriate genre
- taking a risk that shows writer's personality

Word Choice:

- striking words and phrases
- specific nouns (i.e., proper nouns)
- active verbs
- descriptive adjectives (also such techniques as hyphenated adjectives)
- specific, accurate words, and striking words (the "right" word)
- figurative language to create images (each type as a separate focus lesson)
- sound devices (each type as a separate focus lesson)
- jargon; appropriate terminology; disciplinary words
- lack of redundancy, wordiness, vagueness, clichés

Sentence Fluency:

- creating well-crafted and well-structured sentences
- variation in sentence types (simple, compound, complex, compound-complex)

- variation in sentence lengths (adding appositives, prepositional phrases, sentence combining, sentence dividing)
- variations in sentence beginnings
- natural cadence and smooth and rhythmic "flow" of sentences
- purposeful rule-breaking for effect (e.g., fragments)

Each of these topics is appropriate for focus lessons in any grade level. For example, more basic writers can be introduced to linking words, then transitional words; proficient writers can become acquainted with transitional phrases; and the more advanced writers can practice the use of transitional sentences or ideas.

Many topics lend themselves to multiple lessons. For example, there are many types of figurative language that can be employed in writing: imagery, similes, metaphors, idioms, personification, and hyperbole. Each type of figurative language would cover at least one focus lesson for one writing. And teachers can build on these lessons through a horizontal curriculum of writings through the year, as well as a vertical curriculum through the years.

FOCUS LESSONS AND REVISITING MENTOR TEXTS

As students learn to employ different traits in focus lessons, they can return to mentor texts used earlier in the memoir unit to look for examples of ideas, structure, and craft, again reading like writers. For example, in a lesson on reflective endings, as their focus lesson mentor-text read-aloud, teachers can revisit the ending of "Where I'm From" (Lyon, 1999) (see Chapter 9).

I am from those moments—
snapped before I budded—
leaf-fall from the family tree

And writers can discuss how Cynthia Rylant (1993) chose to conclude *When I Was Young in the Mountains* (see Chapter 9).

When I was young in the mountains, I never wanted to go to the ocean, and I never wanted to go to the desert. I never wanted to go anywhere else in the world, for I was in the mountains. And that was always enough.

In this lesson, as the Teacher Model, teachers add reflective endings to their own memoir drafts, thinking aloud as they compose. Example: Roessing, "Back in the 'Hood"(see Chapter 9).

I am from a small town and tree-filled yards,
Family dinners, barbecuing, and birthday parties,
Storing memories to build big dreams—
Endless with possibilities.

In small groups students can be given a short text, either real or fictitious, to which they add a reflective ending as a Guided Practice. Since they are not the author of the text, it may be difficult to actually reflect on the incident. It would be more effective to use a text where they are familiar with the writer, such as a diary entry by Anne Frank or someone they have studied in history, but even using a nursery rhyme, such as "Mary Had a Little Lamb," many students could practice creating a reflection from the character's point of view.

This also would be a fitting opportunity for readers to look back at the memoirs they read independently (for examples of reflective endings of the memoir or conclusions of individual events within the memoir) to evaluate craft and structure, continuing to read like writers. This activity can be accomplished with any focus lesson.

EDITING FOR CONVENTIONS

Many students confuse revision and editing. Editing is done to prepare the writing for publication or public viewing, by proofreading and correcting to conform to the conventions or standards of the style and form in which the text is written. Editing takes place after the piece is drafted and fully revised. It serves no purpose to edit text that may be removed or revised. Editing includes correcting punctuation, spelling, and capitalization, applying grammar and usage rules, and proofreading for mistakes. When teaching conventions, teachers should teach the reasoning behind each convention.

And, like all focus lessons, it is only effective to teach one convention at a time. Teachers should not expect writers to correct everything. For example, in one writing the editing focus lesson could be the comma rule for punctuating items in a series. Depending on the level of prior knowledge and learning, teachers may begin with single items in a series and move to multiple items or phrases and clauses in a series prior to progressing to other conventions. The convention lesson that follows could be another comma rule, a different punctuation rule, or subject-verb agreement. Many convention lessons can be taken from the Common Core Language Standards.

An additional suggestion concerns peer editing. Writers should work together in pairs to peer edit the writings of each writer; students should not trade papers. It is also difficult to edit one's own writing; working together and reading aloud limits seeing what writers *thought* they wrote.

Keep in mind the goal of editing for conventions: Does the lack or misuse of conventions interfere with reading and understanding? Teachers (and parents) need to remember that Conventions is only *one* of the traits. If a writing is going to be on public display, either the teacher can perform a final editing or a note can be displayed with the editing lessons that have been covered. Not all writers have been *taught* all conventions by the time they reach a particular grade level.

Teachers can plan focus lessons within writings, across writings, within and across units, and across the year.

ASSESSMENT: USING A TRAIT RUBRIC

How can teachers assess these very personal writings? The key is to assess objectively with rubrics that assess only what has been taught. When teachers grade for everything, for skills that have not been taught, or for which writers are individually not developmentally ready, students will learn to play it safe. They will only employ techniques they are sure they can get "right." We want to reward risk taking in writing, or writers will never grow, and their writing will remain innocuous, voiceless, and formulaic.

For example, if one focus lesson has been taught for each domain, the rubric for the writing might look like the following:

___/50 pts Content: 5 childhood topics or 25 specific details about 1 topic (*Brainstorming Lesson*)

___/10 pts Organization: a reflective conclusion (*Revision Lesson 2*)

___/20 pts Voice: proper nouns (4 identified by writer) (*Revision Lesson 1*)

___/10 pts Conventions:

    ___/5 pts proper use of commas in items in a series (2 identified by writer) (*Editing Lesson*)

    ___/5 pts writing is proofread

___/10 pts Past Skills*: demonstrates effective use of focus-lesson skill(s) from past writings

One may notice that this rubric assesses for only lessons that have been taught for this writing by the teacher. Topics were gathered by means of the brainstorming discussions, gathered on organizing maps or charts, and based on concepts from the mentor text(s). The two revision lessons are reflected, as is the one conventions lesson. The rubric allows for experimentation and growth.

A rubric such as this allows for flexibility in grading for differentiation. For example, depending how *topics* is identified in the teaching, teachers may expect their more proficient students to further develop each topic, such as expanding their "activities" with a mention of a variety of types of activities, such as clubs, sports, and games. For the more emergent writers, credit may be given if five topics were included, but each topic was less developed. If students only wrote about one topic, they can be expected to have a number of details that can be differentiated.

Five points could be given for a conclusion that fit the definition of a conclusion and made an effective transition from the body of the writing but was not "reflective," while some adolescents are affectively more reflective or better critical thinkers than others.

Quantifying a minimum expectation, such as "four proper nouns," prevents writers from overusing a technique, thereby reducing the effectiveness of the technique, just to gain points; requiring that writers identify the trait in the writing ascertains that the craft was used purposefully. Limiting a requirement (two proper uses of items in a series) prevents teachers from suppressing the writer's creativity or manipulating writings into becoming just another worksheet.

Instead of, or in addition to, "proofreading" as a convention, teachers may want to require, as a percentage of the convention points, that the piece follow the conventions of the chosen genre.

*Most rubrics ignore improvement in skills already taught. The teacher or writers can determine which skill(s) taught in past writing the writer can also focus on in the current writing. "Effective use" of past skills is considered, rather than improvement, so as not to penalize proficient writers. However, if teachers would rather give points to evolving writers for continuing to improve a past skill, they may wish to give those same points to proficient writers for trying a new technique or, as CCSS Writing Anchor Standard 5 suggests, "trying a new approach." An emphasis on reconsidering past skills could also be handled through extra credit points.

This rubric is merely a model and should be revised to reflect each assignment and learning expectations. However the rubric is designed, it needs to be equally applicable to writings in any genre, from prose narratives to graphic essays to list poetry, as should all the focus lessons. And students should discuss and have copies of the rubric prior to final revision.

ASSESSMENT: USING A CHARACTERISTICS RUBRIC

Another type of rubric would be to create a checklist from a combination of the two lists the class developed in this unit, some of which overlap:

"Features of a Good Memoir List" (Chapter 2)

- is based on memories
- is about small moments—focuses on one thing—one race, one street football game
- has very specific details and names
- has descriptions
- has humor
- has dialogue
- readers can hear the different voices (ways of talking) of the different speakers
- has dialect
- gives background information—audience awareness
- topics relate to the audience's common interests and experiences
- makes a point
- a variety of characters are included in the stories—not just the narrator
- has metaphors and similes
- has hyperbole
- uses onomatopoeia
- has personification
- has flashbacks

"Characteristics of Good Writing" (Chapter 10)

- has a compelling lead
- has a reflective, thought-provoking conclusion
- has an organizational pattern
- uses specific details, such as proper nouns
- uses examples and elaboration
- uses active verbs
- has imagery—sensory details
- has vivid characters and settings
- has figurative language
    metaphor and simile
    personification
    hyperbole
    oxymoron
- uses speech
    dialogue
    thoughts
    colloquialisms: dialect and slang
- uses sound devices
    onomatopoeia
    alliteration
- uses repetition
- has a variety of sentence structures

Students could gather points from including, or attempting, a certain number of the features or traits, but if a technique has not been directly taught, students could identify what they incorporated and some sort of credit should be given for the attempt.

Students could also be involved in rubric creation for these writings. In that way, writers are discussing and determining the criteria on which writing should be evaluated and weighing the relative merits of the features of writing.

PUBLICATION

The final determinations writers make are how to publish their writings. Not all writers will want to share all writings with the public at large but generally value having an audience for their writings.

If writers have completed, revised, and edited more than one piece, they may decide to share only one publication, share different writings with different audiences, or design a comprehensive venue or repository for sharing all the completed writings. Writers may

- share with friends and/or families
- save for future friends and families
- publish in a class book
- perform for classmates and guests

- design and create an individual publication; for example,

  create a collage of works,

  scrapbook the writing, embellishing appropriately, or

  design an artifact or "time capsule" in which to store the writings

John combined and sequenced his three different memoirs, including "Ode to the Baseball Glove" in a scrapbook titled "A Boy's Life." Jen placed each of her writings in a container or small plastic bag and stored all three in her favorite childhood lunchbox for her future family.

Sometimes writers would rather share their stories orally, perform their writings, or present them in a technological program or platform, possibly a program as simple as PowerPoint, integrating the Speaking and Listening Standards.

REFLECTION

Even though memoir itself is reflective, it is beneficial for students to analyze and reflect on their process and progress through this unit. After students complete and publish or perform their writings, they ponder the aspects of the project.

1. What do you see as the value of writing memoirs?
2. What do you see as the value of reading memoirs?
3. What do you see as the value of reading memoirs while writing memoirs?
4. What was your favorite brainstorming activity? Why?
5. What brainstorming activity was the most effective in helping you to gather memories?
6. What was your favorite writing and why?
7. Tim O'Brien said, "You don't have to tell a true story to tell the truth." Please share the story behind one of your stories. What was the "truth" that your writing shared?
8. What was your favorite genre to read and/or write or technology platform to try?
9. How did your writing change during this unit?
   a. from reading mentor texts?
   b. from watching teacher modeling?
   c. from seeing student samples?
10. What was easy? What was challenging?
11. What surprised you or how did you surprise yourself?
12. What might you do differently if you were to write a memoir again?
13. What can you take from this unit to other types of writing throughout the year?
14. What do you consider your best writing, and on what criteria would you base that claim?

In their reflections, students generally will not only focus on their memoir readings and writings but will consider the writing *and* reading strategies and techniques they have gained. They will realize that, as "creative nonfiction," memoir writing combines narrative and informative writing processes (such as figurative language and experiential research techniques, just as memoir reading combines fiction and nonfiction reading strategies such as following plot while gathering information) and that this unit has likewise bridged the gap between writing and reading.

CONCLUSION

Where We Have Been and
Where We Can Go from Here

READING MEMOIRS ACROSS THE CURRICULUM

Throughout this unit, students have been reading memoirs, but they have also generally learned to read like writers and have gained critical reading skills applicable to reading all texts. They have expanded their reading strategies and skills, which will transfer to other readings—notably research reading—in all disciplines.

Prior to, but at least by the time of completion of their memoir writings, students will have finished reading at least one full-length memoir. As a critical reading activity as well as for effecting closure to the literary portion of the unit, readers should reflect on their reading. It is vital to train developing readers to return to the text for greater comprehension and interpretation to move students beyond literal understanding of complex text. "Each rereading of a text gives readers a greater and deeper understanding, making them better readers and increasing comprehension" (Roessing, 2009). Critical readers are reflective readers.

RELATING TO OTHER MEMOIRISTS

Now that students have examined their pasts to write memoirs, it is valuable to guide students to connect their experiences with those of other memoirists, implementing the compare-contrast structure so necessary for students to learn:

- CCSS ELA-Literacy.W.6.2a and W.7.2a Introduce a topic; organize ideas, concepts, and information, using strategies such as . . . comparison/contrast, and cause/effect; include formatting (e.g., headings), graphics (e.g., charts, tables), and multimedia when useful to aiding comprehension.

Looking at "their" memoirists' writing and determining categories to compare, students examine their own pasts and contemplate the universality of experiences. They are also making connections, or bridging the gap, between themselves and those who may originate from different cultures: nationality, ethnicity, race, age, gender, religion, geography, and/or socioeconomic status and times.

A creative and applicable format for compare/contrast structure—one that has not been discussed in this unit thus far—is poetry in two voices, a genre that facilitates analyzing and evaluating similarities and differences. In poetry in two voices, poets write from two perspectives, comparing and contrasting. Anything that is similar is written directly across from each other and read simultaneously; the contrasting details are written on separate lines and read one at a time, in whatever order the author deems most effective. This type of poem is meant to be read aloud by two people; it is an aural experience and can be very powerful when the two voices enter in unison, stressing similarities. Read silently, it becomes a visual experience (Roessing, 2009, 2013).

Table 13.1. Teenagers

Being a teenager was hard in the Sixties.	Being a teenager was hard in the Sixties.
I was a European-American girl.	I was a Puerto Rican girl.
I grew up in western Pennsylvania.	I grew up in Puerto Rico
in a small town.	in a small village.
We never moved from Pennsylvania	We moved back and forth many times;
	We finally came to New York
We were the *hicks.*	We were *jibaro.*
But my father made a good living;	*My* father could barely support us;
At heart he was an artist.	Although he was a poet.
In school I never felt the same as everybody else.	In school I never felt the same as everybody else.
"Jew."	"Spic"
But in high school I did well.	But in high school I did well.
Academics were important to me.	Academics were important to me.
I liked attention and to perform which caused me to become a teacher and a writer.	I liked attention and to perform which caused me to become a writer.
We are both storytellers, telling the stories of ourselves and others.	We are both storytellers, telling the stories of ourselves and others.

Reading the memoir *When I Was Puerto Rican* by Esmeralda Santiago (Santiago, 1998), an author reflected on both Ms. Santiago's past and her own and created "Teenagers, a Poem in Two Voices" (Roessing, 2012):

Analyzing the model poem, students notice that

- the two women share many commonalities: age, gender, nationality, members of minority groups, professions, education, intelligence; and
- the two women also have cultural differences: ethnicity, religion, socioeconomic level, geography.

What is crucial in this endeavor is that the text, in this case the memoir read, is examined critically and then the student's memoirs become texts that are also surveyed and studied reflectively during the creation of this new, integrated writing, the two-voice poem. In a cursory observation, the author might have thought she had nothing in common with a young girl from Puerto Rico, but upon closer inspection, the author discerned many commonalities. The exercise revealed what the people, places, and events in her own life meant on a more comprehensive, global scale.

This pursuit would be particularly beneficial in preparing readers to meet Common Core standards of integration of knowledge and ideas, such as CCSS.ELA-Literacy.RI6.9, applicable to reading informational texts in sixth grade, to "compare and contrast one author's presentation of events with that of another (e.g., a memoir written by and a biography on the same person)," while seventh graders prepare to "analyze how two or more authors writing about the same topic shape their presentations of key information by emphasizing different evidence or advancing different interpretations of facts" (CCSS. ELA-Literacy.RI7.9), progressing to comparing topics and themes in divergent texts.

EXTENDING MEMOIR READING INTO CONTENT AREA CLASSROOMS

Memoirs in Mathematics Class

To integrate reading in a discipline, rather than reading research articles or biographies about people who contributed to that field or have something to share about the subject matter, it is more effective for students to read their memoirs. Nothing is more powerful than hearing a person's own voice (see Appendix B).

In mathematics classes, students could read memoirs by mathematicians or those whose lives were affected or impacted by mathematics. Some examples are *The Crossing of Heaven: Memoirs of a Mathematician* by Karl Gustafson, *The Fractalist: Memoir of a Scientific Maverick* by Benoit Mandelbrot, or *Fascinating Mathematical People: Interviews and Memoirs,* edited by Donald J. Albers and Gerald L. Alexanderson. Younger students could read and discuss Samantha Abeel's memoir about her dyscalculia, *My Thirteenth Winter.*

Memoirs in Science Classes

In science class, individual students could read memoirs of scientists and inventors, such as Homer Hickam's *Rocket Boys* or *An Astronaut's Guide to Life on Earth* by astronaut Chris Hadfield.

However, developing biologists and zoologists could meet in topical book clubs, reading

- *Part of the Pride: My Life Among the Big Cats of Africa* by animal behaviorist Kevin Richardson;
- *The Elephant Whisperer: My Life with the Herd in the African Wild* by conservationist Lawrence Anthony;
- *Tippi: My Book of Africa,* Tippi Degre's memoir;
- *Tales of an African Vet* written by Roy Aronson; and
- *All Creatures Great and Small* by British veterinarian James Herriot (or one of Herriot's other memoirs).

In a general science class, book clubs could read memoirs by scientists in divergent fields or by memoirists whose lives were affected in some way by science or scientific principles.

Memoirs in Social Studies/History Classes

Many diverse memoirs have been written by people involved in significant historic events, reporting from their points of view. There are numerous books and memoirs written by those involved in the Holocaust. The majority of these accounts were written after the war by survivors and, consequently, are truly reflective memoirs, but there are also those actual diaries written *during* the war such as those kept by Anne Frank and Hannah Senesh. There are memoirs by victims—Jews and non-Jews, by rescuers, by those who took part in the Resistance, and even a few memoirs written by former Hitler Youth members.

Book clubs can each focus on one of these perspectives and, after reading and discussion meetings within the individual book clubs, the book club members collectively compare their perceptions.

- CCRA.ELA-Literacy.R6 Assess how point of view or purpose shapes the content and style of a text.
- CCRA.ELA-Literacy.R9 Analyze how two or more texts address similar themes or topics in order to build knowledge or to compare the approaches the authors take.

Alternatively, book clubs can be formed around memoirs written by those involved in diverse issues or disparate time periods—historical and current—and locales. Many of these titles are listed in Appendix B. Some examples are:

- *Kaffir Boy,* Mark Mathabane's recounting of growing up in South Africa under Apartheid;
- *Persepolis,* Marjane Satrapi's description of Iranian life before, during, and after the 1979 revolution;
- *I Am Malala* by a Pakistani, Malala Yousafzai, shot by the Talaban for fighting for an education;
- *A Long Way Gone, Memoirs of a Boy Soldier* by Ishmael Beah, a boy soldier in Sierra Leone's civil war;
- *Through My Eyes,* Ruby Bridges's account of school integration in Louisiana;
- *Zlata's Diary: A Child's Life in Wartime Sarajevo,* Zlata Filipovic's firsthand 1991–1993 account of civil war in Bosnia; and one of the many memoirs of the Holocaust.

Following book club readings and discussions, this would present an appropriate opportunity for the readers to form groups, comprised of one representative from each book club, to write "poetry in multiple voices" or another type of multiple-perspective writing, such as a play where the memoirists meet in a fictitious setting, possibly a global human rights summit.

If disciplinary teachers cannot allocate time necessary for reading memoirs, they could either pair with an English/Language Arts teacher for an interdisciplinary unit or incorporate excerpts of memoirs into their curricula.

EXTENDING MEMOIR WRITING INTO CONTENT AREA CLASSROOMS

While writers are writing their memoirs, they are learning writing strategies and skills that they can apply to any writing in any mode or format in all disciplines, and they have learned to experiment with writing. Writers have analyzed and evaluated the characteristics of good writing and have applied them in their own writings. Writers will now write in narrative, informational, and argument modes on disparate topics with more organization, style, and voice, and with audience and purpose in mind. Effective writing is effective writing in any discipline, even though many times there are disparate disciplinary guidelines and procedures.

In writing memoir, memoirists have learned to conduct research. Using experiential sources and, in some cases, interviews, artifacts, and written evidence, they have learned how to gather facts, interpret events, and organize details; they have determined which information to use and how to use it, which details are relevant, which interpretations are accurate, and which memories are reliable, all higher-level research strategies. Additionally, student researchers have learned to acknowledge bias in reporting, even though the bias may be their own.

Developing writers have learned how to support stories with information and, conversely, how to take information and turn it into narratives. They have perceived that life is a series of stories and those stories determine who they have become; they have acknowledged the importance of story. "If a nation loses its storytellers, it loses its childhood" (Peter Handke).

But how specifically can memoir writing extend into the content-area classrooms?

Students can research and write memoirs of historic figures in social studies classes, artists in art class, scientists and mathematicians in the related disciplines, or of those people who contributed to any disciplinary field, even health and physical education—meeting Common Core State Standards in ELA-Literacy, including Grades 6–12 Literacy in History/Social Studies, Science, and Technical Subjects.

- CCRA.ELA-Literacy.W7 Conduct short as well as more sustained research projects based on focused questions, demonstrating understanding of the subject under investigation.
- CCRA.ELA-Literacy.W8 Gather relevant information from multiple print and digital sources, assess the credibility and accuracy of each source, and integrate the information while avoiding plagiarism.
- CCRA.ELA-Literacy.W9 Draw evidence from literary or informational texts to support analysis, reflection, and research.

This endeavor necessitates a more analytical and creative approach than simply writing biographies as students recount events in the subjects' lives or their accomplishments and what influences in their pasts led to these accomplishments from the viewpoint of these people. The next step would be to reflect back on those accomplishments and their impact on society, again, as much as possible, determining the subject's perspective.

Memoirs about Past Academic Experiences

After having the opportunity to study and write memoirs on a variety of topics, students can employ a practical approach in their classes in other disciplines. Teachers can invite students to reflect on and relate their histories and past relationships with that particular content—math, for example—and write their own subject-matter memoirs (e.g., "Seven Years of Struggle with Math," "Awesome Achievements in Art," or "Ups & Downs Throughout My History in History Class").

There are many memoir-type texts, such as Jane Kenyon's "Trouble with Math in a One-Room Country School" (Chapter 9), that would serve as appropriate mentors. It is advantageous for students in any discipline to look back on their earlier experiences with a subject, analyzing their current mindset and perceptions. This activity also allows the teacher to become aware of their students' levels of content-area confidence and the origins of their current attitudes toward their own competencies in certain academic pursuits.

A Model

Students can model informative disciplinary writings that reveals information learned or researched after any of the mentor texts employed in the memoir unit. The model below is based on the "When I Was Young in . . ." samples in Chapter 9. It was written in the format of a free-verse poem; however, it also includes one rhyming couplet, the rhythm illustrating the ease of the life that "should have been." What students should note is the research that was conducted to supplement the information learned in the history class.

When I Was Young in Warsaw, 1940

When I was young in Warsaw,
Nazi troops invaded our city.
It was 1940 and
They sent my family to live inside a ghetto,
A small town surrounded by a gate.

The ghetto became more and more crowded
As over 400,000 people were forced in.
Our fathers were not allowed to work, and
Food became more and more scarce.

When I was young in Warsaw,
Life, as we once knew it, stopped.
Instead of "Prosze," we heard "Schnell!"
Desperately we tried to stay alive,
Just because we were Jews.

1942, a few at a time we were marched away
And taken to a train which was more crowded
Than even our ghetto.
People died, standing up.

When I was young in Warsaw
I was taken away from Warsaw—one of 265,000.
Away from my friends, away from my relatives,
Away from celebrating the Sabbath in our own way.

Existing in a camp with a bigger gate,
Bigger than that around our ghetto,

Separated from my mother.
Soldiers surrounded us – men with guns...
We didn't survive very long in Treblinka.

When I was young in Warsaw,
Life should have continued
as it was meant to be.
I should have grown up, had a family and wife,
A job, a religion, and a long, long life.
I should have grown old in Warsaw.

But most importantly, as with reading memoirs, as students have been writing memoirs, they also have learned in general the crafts of writing and have gained effective writing skills applicable to writing in all disciplines.

HAVING BRIDGED THE GAP

Students no longer categorize text as fiction or nonfiction, writing as narrative or informational, or perceive a Great Divide between reading and writing, raising their potential and gaining proficiency. Students become better readers by reading and writing and become better writers by writing and reading, and with the inclusion of choice, time, and appropriate mentors and high-interest lessons to ease their way, they *will* participate in both, becoming more proficient in literacy. As they bridge those gaps through memoir, they also bridge gaps between themselves and others, their pasts and their futures, to reach their core.

APPENDIX A
Resources for Teachers

MENTOR TEXTS AND MEMOIR COLLECTIONS

Chapter 1: Defining & Gathering Memories

Fox, Mem. *Wilfred Gordon McDonald Partridge*. New York: Puffin Books, 1992. [picture book]

Woodson, Jacqueline. *Sweet, Sweet Memory*. New York: Jump at the Sun/Hyperion for Children, 2000. [picture book]

Chapter 2: From Memories to Memoir

Collins, Billy. "The Lanyard." ***The Trouble with Poetry** and Other Poems*. New York: Random House, 2005. [poem]

Paulsen, Gary. "Introduction." *Shelf Talk: Stories by the Book*. Simon & Schuster for Young Readers, 2003. [excerpt]

Chapter 3: Reading Memoirs: Reading Like a Writer

Mah, Adeline Yen. *Chinese Cinderella: The True Story of an Unwanted Daughter*. New York: Dell Laurel-Leaf, 1999. [novel-length memoir]

Chapter 4: Memoirs of Time & Age

Collins, Billy. "On Turning Ten." **Art of Drowning**. Pittsburgh: University of Pittsburgh Press, 1995. [poem]

Stafford, William. "What's In My Journal?" *Crossing Unmarked Snow: Further Views on the Writer's Vocation*. Ann Arbor: University of Michigan, 1998. [poem]

Stafford, William. "Things I Learned Last Week." *Sound of the Ax: Aphorism and Poems by William Stafford*. Eds. Vincent Wixon and Paul Merchant. Pittsburgh: University of Pittsburgh Press, 2014. [poem]

Vinz, Mark. "What I Remember About Sixth Grade." *Late Night Calls*. Moorhead, MN: NewRivers Press, 1992. [poem].

Chapter 5: Memoirs of Objects & Mementoes

Dahl, Roald. *Boy*. New York: Farrar, Straus And Giroux, 1986. [excerpt]

Nerudo, Pablo. "Ode to the Tomato." *Neruda, Selected Poems*. New York: Houghton Mifflin, 1990. [poem]

Osborne, Mary Pope. "All Ball." *When I was Your Age: Original Stories About Growing Up, Volume One*. Ed. Amy Ehrlich. Cambridge, MA: Candlewick Press, 1996. [personal narrative]

Parton, Dolly. "Coat of Many Colors." *Coat of Many Colors*. RCA Records. 1971. [CD]

Parton, Dolly. *Coat of Many Colors*. New York: HarperCollins, 1996 [book]

Polacco, Patricia. *The Keeping Quilt*. New York: Simon & Schuster for Young Readers, 1988. [picture book]

Rylant, Cynthia. "Wax Lips." *Waiting to Waltz: A Childhood.* New York: Atheneum/Richard Jackson Books, 2001. [poem]

Soto, Gary. "Ode to Pablo's Tennis Shoes." *Neighborhood Odes.* New York: Harcourt, Inc., 2005. [poem]

Chapter 6: Memoirs of Places

Bouchard, David. *If you're not from the prairie...* New York: Aladdin Paperbacks, 1998. [poem picture book]

Giovanni, Nikki. *Knoxville, Tennessee.* Scholastic, 1994. [poem picture book]

Goldstein, Kenneth Roy. "Notes from the Past—A Memoir." *Aaron's Intifada And Other Short Stories.* Lincoln, NE: iUniverse, 2002. [personal narrative]

Mori, Kyoto. "Learning to Swim." *When I was Your Age: Original Stories About Growing Up, Volume Two.* Ed. Amy Ehrlich. Cambridge, MA: Candlewick Press, 2002. [personal narrative]

Rylant, Cynthia. *Waiting to Waltz: A Childhood.* New York: Atheneum/Richard Jackson Books, 2001. [poetry collection]

Schotter, Roni. *Nothing Ever Happens on 90th Street.* New York: Scholastic, 1999. [picture book]

Chapter 7: Memoirs of People and Relationships

Hopkins, Lee Bennett. *Been to Yesterdays: Poems of a Life.* Honesdale, PA: Wordsong, 1995.

Leigh, Richard C and Martine, Layng, Jr. "The Greatest Man I Never Knew." McEntire, Reba. *For My Broken Heart.* MCA Records, 1991.[song]

Micklos, John. *Grandparent Poems.* Honesdale, PA: Wordsong, 2004. [poetry collection]

Rylant, Cynthia. *The Relatives Came.* New York: Aladdin, 1985. [picture book]

Sones, Sonya. *Stop Pretending: What Happened When My Big Sister Went Crazy.* New York: HarperTempest, 1999. [verse novel-length memoir]

Yolen, Jane. "The Long Closet." Ehrlich, Amy, ed. *When I Was Your Age: Original Stories About Growing Up, Volume Two.* Cambridge, MA: Candlewick Press, 2002. [personal memoir]

Chapter 8: Memoirs of Crises and Defining Moments or Events

Audet, Cynthia. "Scar." *The Sun.* January 2003. [magazine article]

Kenyon, Jane. "Trouble with Math in a One-room Country School." *Collected Poems.* Minneapolis, MN: Graywolf Press, 2005. [poem]

Rockwell, Norman. *The Discovery.* 1956. Norman Rockwell Museum, Stockbridge, MA. [painting]

Viorst, Judith. "Since Hannah Moved Away." *If I Were in Charge of the World and Other Worries.* New York: Macmillan, 1981. [poem]

Webb, Charles. "The Death of Santa Claus." *Reading the Water.* Boston: Northeastern University Press, 2001. [poem]

Chapter 9: Memoirs of Where We Are From

Bradby, Marie. *Momma, Where Are You From?* New York: Orchard, 2000. [picture book}

Cisneros, Sandra. "Eleven." *Woman Hollering Creek.* New York: Vintage, 1992. [short story]

Lyon, George Ella. "Where I'm From." *Where I'm From, Where Poems Come From.* Spring, TX: Absey & Company, Inc., 1999. [poem]

Roessing, Lesley. "Back in the Hood." *No More "Us" and "Them": Classroom Lessons & Activities to Promote Peer Respect.* Lanham, Md: Rowman & Littlefield, 2012. [poem]

Rylant, Cynthia. *When I Was Young in the Mountains.* New York: Penguin Group, 1993. [picture book]

Chapter 10: Analyzing Memoir Writing: Learning from Mentor Texts

Holahan, David. "When Lobsters Run Free." *Philadelphia Inquirer*, April 23, 2006. [newsarticle]

Polacco, Patricia. *Betty Doll.* New York: Philomel, 2001. [picture book]

Polacco, Patricia. *Meteor.* New York: Puffin, 1996. [picture book]

Polacco, Patricia. *My Ol' Man.* New York: Puffin, 1999. [picture book]
Polacco, Patricia. *My Rotten Redheaded Older Brother.* New York: Aladdin, 1994. [picture book]
Polacco, Patricia. *Some Birthday!* New York: Simon & Schuster, 1993. [picture book]
Polacco, Patricia. *Thundercake.* New York: Puffin, 1997. [picture book]

Chapter 11: Genre Choice: Making the Form Fit the Function

Bridges, Ruby. *Through My Eyes.* New York: Scholastic Press, 1999.
Kim, Derek Kirk. "Hurdles." *Same Difference and Other Stories.* Marietta, GA: Top Shelf Productions, 2004. [graphic]
Satrapi, Marjane. *Persepolis: The Story of a Childhood.* New York: Pantheon Books, 2004. [novel-length memoir]
Spiegelman, Art. "Eye Ball." *Breakdowns: Portrait of the Artist as a Young %@&*!* New York: Pantheon, 2008. [graphic]

MEMOIR AND PERSONAL ESSAY COLLECTIONS

Texts from the following collections can supplement or replace mentor texts listed.

Curry, Boykin, Kasbar, Brian, and Baer, Emily Angel eds. *Essays That Worked for College Applications: 50 Essays from Successful Applications to the Nation's Top Colleges.* New York: Ballatine Books, 2003.
Dillard, Annie and Conley, Cort, eds. *Modern American Memoirs.* New York: HarperPerennial, 1996.
Ehrlich, Amy, ed. *When I Was Your Age: Original Stories About Growing Up, Volume One.*
Ehrlich, Amy, ed. *When I Was Your Age: Original Stories About Growing Up, Volume Two.*
Fershleiser, Rachel and Smith, Larry. *I Can't Keep My Own Secrets: Six-Word Memoirs by Teens Famous & Obscure.* New York: HarperTeen, 2009.
Friedman, Ina R. *The Other Victims: First Person Stories of Non-Jews Persecuted by the Nazis.* New York: HMH Books for Young Readers, 1995.
Hall, Megan Kelley and Jones, Carrie, eds. *Dear Bully: Seventy Authors Tell Their Stories.* New York: HarperTeen, 2011.
The Harvard Independent. *100 Successful College Application Essays, Third Edition.* New York: New American Library, 2013.
"Lives." *New York Times Magazine.* A weekly column featuring personal narratives by professional and amateur writers. *http://topics.nytimes.com/top/features/magazine/columns/lives/*
Mazer, Anne, ed. *Going Where I'm Coming From: A Memoirs of American Youth.* New York: Persea Books, 1995.
Scieszka, John. Guys *Write for Guys Read: Boys' Favorite Authors Write About Being Boys.* New York: Viking, 2008.
Youth Communication. *Starting With "I": Personal Essays by Teenagers.* New York: Persea Books, 1997.

APPENDIX B

Resources for Readers

MEMOIRS FOR WHOLE-CLASS, BOOK CLUB, OR INDEPENDENT READING

Abeel, Samantha. *My Thirteenth Winter, a Memoir.* New York: Scholastic, 2003.

Albers, Donald J. and Alexanderson, Gerald L., Eds. *Fascinating Mathematical People: Interviews and Memoirs.* Princeton, NJ: Princeton University Press, 2011.

Albom, Mitch. *Tuesdays with Morrie: An Old Man, a Young Man, and Life's Greatest Lesson.* New York: Broadway Books, 2002.

*Angelou, Maya. *I Know Why the Caged Bird Sings.* New York: Bantam Books, 1993.

Anonymous. *Go Ask Alice.* New York: Simon Pulse, 1998.

Anthony, Lawrence. *The Elephant Whisperer: My Life with the Herd in the African Wild.* New York: St. Martin's Griffin, 2012.

Appelt, Kathi. *My Father's Summers: A Daughter's Memoir.* New York: Henry Holt and Company, 2004.

Appleman-Jurman, Alicia. *Alicia: My Story.* New York: Bantam Books, 1988.

Aronson, Roy. *Tales of an African Vet.* Guilford, CT: Lyons Press, 2011.

Ashe, Arthur. *Days of Grace.* New York: Ballantine Books, 1993.

Bagdasarian, Adam. *First French Kiss: and Other Traumas.* New York: Farrar, Straus and Giroux, 2002.

Beah, Ishmael. *A Long Way Gone: Memoirs of a Boy Soldier.* New York: Sarah Crichton Books, 2007.

Beals, Melba. *Warriors Don't Cry.* New York: Simon Pulse, 2007.

Berenstain, Stan and Berenstain, Jan. *Down a Sunny Dirt Road.* New York: Random House Books for Young Readers, 2002.

Bernall, Misty. *She Said Yes: The Unlikely Martyrdom of Cassie Bernall.* New York: Pocket, 1999.

Biederman, Alyssa. *My Rory: A Personal Journey Through Teenage Anorexia.* Lincoln, NE: iUniverse, 2005.

Blanco, Jodee. *Please Stop Laughing at Me . . . One Woman's Inspirational Story.* Avon, MA: Adams Media, 2010.

Booker, Sheri. *Nine Years Under: Coming of Age in an Inner-City Funeral Home.* New York: Gotham Books, 2013.

Breashears, David. *High Exposure: An Enduring Passion for Everest and Unforgiving Places.* New York: Simon and Schuster Paperbacks, 1999.

Bridges, Ruby. *Through My Eyes.* New York: Scholastic Press, 1999.

Britton-Jackson, Livia. *I Have Lived a Thousand Years: Growing up in the Holocaust.* New York: Simon Pulse, 1999.

Britton-Jackson, Livia. *My Bridges of Hope: Searching for Life and Love after Auschwitz.* New York, Simon Pulse. 2002

Bryson, Bill. *A Walk in the Woods: Rediscovering America on the Appalachian Trail.* New York: Broadway Books, 1998.

Buergenthal, Thomas. *A Lucky Child: A Memoir of Surviving Auschwitz as a Young Boy.* New York: Back Bay Books, 2010.

Bulla, Clyde. *A Grain of Wheat: A Writer Begins.* Honesdale, PA: Boyds Mills Press, 2005.

Byers, Betsy. *The Moon and I.* New York: HarperCollins, 1996.

Carter, Forrest. *The Education of Little Tree.* Albuquerque: University of New Mexico Press, 1999.

Cleary, Beverly. *A Girl from Yamhill.* New York: HarperCollins, 1996.

Cleary, Beverly. *My Own Two Feet: A Memoir.* New York: HarperCollins, 1996.

Codell, Esme Raji. *Sing a Song of Tuna Fish: A Memoir of My Fifth-Grade Year.* New York: Hyperion, 2006.

Comaneci, Nadia. *Letters to a Young Gymnast.* New York: Basic Books, 2004.

Conroy, Frank. *Stop Time: A Memoir*. New York, Penguin Books, 1977.

Corrigan, Eireann. *You Remind Me of You: A Poetry Memoir*. New York: Scholastic, 2002.

Coughlin, Gunnery Sgt. Jack, USMC; and Kuhlman, Capt. Casey, USMCR. *Shooter: The Autobiography of the Top-Ranked Marine Sniper*. New York: St. Martin's Press, 2005.

Cox, Lynne. *Swimming to Antarctica: Tales of a Long-Distance Swimmer*. New York: Harcourt, 2004.

Crutcher, Chris. *King of the Mild Frontier: An Ill-Advised Autobiography*. New York: Greenwillow Books, 2003.

Cunningham, Laura Shaine. *Sleeping Arrangements*. New York: Riverhead Books, 1989.

Cunxin, Li. *Mao's Last Dancer*. New York: Berkeley Publishing, 2005.

Dahl, Roald. *Boy: Tales of Childhood*. New York: Puffin, 2009.

Dahl, Roald. *Going Solo*. New York: Puffin Books, 1988.

Davis, Sampson, Jenkins, George and Hunt, Rameck. *The Pact: Three Young Men Make a Promise and Fulfill a Dream*. New York: Riverhead Books, 2003.

Davis, Sampson, Jenkins, George and Hunt, Rameck. *We Beat the Streets: How a Friendship Pact Led to Success*. New York: Puffin Books, 2006.

DeGeneres, Ellen. *My Point . . . And I Do Have One*. New York: Bantam Books, 1995.

Degre, Tippi. *Tippi: My Book of Africa*. Cape Town, South Africa: Random House Struik, 2012.

dePaola, Tomie. *26 Fairmount Avenue*. New York: Putnam Juvenile, 1996.

Diamond, Cheryl. *Model: A Memoir*. New York: Simon Pulse, 2008.

Dillard, Annie. *An American Childhood*. New York: Harper & Row Publishers, 2008.

Dog, Mary Crow. *Lakota Woman*. New York: HarperPerennial, 1991.

*Douglass, Frederick. *Narrative of the Life of Frederick Douglass*. Mineola, NY: Dover Publications, 1995.

Feig, Paul. *Kick Me: Adventures in Adolescence*. New York: Three Rivers Press, 2002.

Fick, Nathaniel. *One Bullet Away: The Making of a Marine Officer*. New York: Houghton Mifflin Co., 2005.

Filipovic, Zlata. *Zlata's Diary: A Child's Life in Wartime Sarajevo*. New York: Penguin Books, 2006.

Fleischman, Sid. *The Abracadabra Kid: A Writer's Life*. New York: Greenwillow Books, 1996.

Fletcher, Ralph. *Marshfield Dreams: When I Was a Kid*. New York: Henry Holt and Company, 2005.

Fox, Michael J. *Lucky Man: A Memoir*. New York: Hyperion, 2003.

Fox, Paula. *Borrowed Finery: A Memoir*. New York: Henry Holt, 2001.

Francis, Melissa. *Diary of a Stage Mother's Daughter: A Memoir*. New York: Weinstein Books, 2012.

Franco, James. *A California Childhood*. San Rafael, CA: Insight Editions, 2013.

*Frank, Anne. *The Diary of a Young Girl*. New York: Anchor Books, 1995.

Freedom Writers and Gruwell, Erin. *The Freedom Writers Diary*. New York: Broadway Books, 2001.

Fritz, Jean. *Homesick: My Own Story*. New York: Putnam Juvenile, 1982.

Gantos, Jack. *Hole in My Life*. New York: Farrar, Straus and Giroux, 2002.

Garner, Eleanor Ramrath. *Eleanor's Story: An American in Hitler's Germany*. New York: Scholastic, 2003.

Gates, Henry Louis, Jr. *Colored People: A Memoir*. New York: Vintage Books, 1995.

George, Jean Craighead. *The Tarantula in My Purse: and 172 Other Wild Pets*. New York: HarperCollins, 1997.

Golabek, Mona. *The Children of Willesden Lane, Beyond the Kindertransport: A Memoir of Music, Love, and Survival*. New York: Warner Books, 2003.

Gottlieb, Lorie. *Stick Figure: A Diary of My Former Self*. New York: Berkley Books, 2000.

Grealy, Lucy. *Autobiography of a Face*. New York: Houghton Mifflin, 1994.

Griffin, John Howard. *Black Like Me*. New York: Penguin Books, 1996.

Grogan, John. *Marley and Me: Life and Love with the World's Worst Dog*. New York: William Morrow, 2006.

Gunther, John. *Death Be Not Proud, a Memoir*. New York: HarperCollins Publishers, 2007.

Gustafson, Karl. *The Crossing of Heaven: Memoirs of a Mathematician*. Heidelberg, Germany: Springer, 2012.

Hadfield, Chris. *An Astronaut's Guide to Life on Earth: What Going to Space Taught Me About Ingenuity, Determination, and Being Prepared for Anything*. New York: Little, Brown and Company, 2013.

Haley, Alex and Malcolm X. *The Autobiography of Malcolm X*. New York: Ballantine Books, 1964.

Hamilton, Bethany. *Soul Surfer: A True Story of Faith, Family, and Fighting to Get Back on the Board*. New York: Pocket Books, 2006.

Hautzig, Deborah. *Second Star to the Right*. New York: Puffin Books, 1999.

Hensel, Jana. *After the Wall: Confessions From an East German Childhood and the Life that Came Next*. New York: Public Affairs, 2004.

Herriot, James. *All Creatures Great and Small*. New York: Bantam Books, 1989.

Hickam, Homer H., Jr. *Rocket Boys*. New York: Dell Publishing, 1998.

Hillman, Laura. *I Will Plant You a Lilac Tree: A Memoir of a Schindler's List Survivor*. New York: Simon Pulse, 2008.

Holliday, Laurel. *Why Do They Hate Me? Young Lives Caught in War and Conflict*. New York: Pocket Books, 1999.

Houston, Jeanne Wakatsuki. *Farewell to Manzanar*. New York: Laurel-Leaf, 2007.

Houze, David. *Twilight People: One Man's Journey to Find His Roots*. Berkeley, CA: University of California Press, 2006.

Hunter, Latoya. *The Diary of Latoya Hunter: My First Year in Junior High*. New York: Vintage, 1993.

Jimenez, Francisco. *Breaking Through*. New York: HMH Books for Young Readers, 2002.

Jimenez, Francisco. *The Circuit: Stories from the Life of a Migrant Child*. Albuquerque: University of New Mexico Press, 1997.

Karr, Mary. *The Liars' Club: A Memoir*. New York: Penguin Books, 2005.

*Katz, Jon. *Geeks: How Two Lost Boys Rode the Internet Out of Idaho*. New York: Broadway Books, 2001.

Kaysen, Susanna. *Girl, Interrupted*. New York: Vintage, 1994.

Kehret, Peg. *Five Pages a Day: A Writer's Journey*. Morton Grove, IL: Albert Whitman & Company, 2002.

Kehret, Peg. *Small Steps: The Year I Got Polio*. Morton Grove, IL: Albert Whitman & Company, 1996.

Kimmel, Haven. *A Girl Named Zippy: Growing Up Small in Mooreland, Indiana*. New York: Broadway Books, 2002.

Knisley, Lucy. *Relish: My Life in the Kitchen*. New York: First Second, 2013.

Levine, Ellen. *Freedom's Children: Young Civil Rights Activists Tell Their Own Stories*. New York: Avon Books, 1994.

Liebster, Simone Arnold. *Facing the Lion: Memoirs of a Young Girl in Nazi Europe*. New Orleans: Grammaton Press, 2000.

Lipiner, Lucy. *Long Journey Home: A Young Girl's Memoir of Surviving the Holocaust*. Bloomington, IN: iUniverse, 2013.

Little, Jean. *Little by Little: A Writer's Education*. New York: Puffin, 1991.

Liu, Na. *Little White Duck: A Childhood in China*. Minneapolis, MN: Graphic Universe, 2012.

Lobel, Anita. *No Pretty Pictures: A Child of War*. New York: Avon Books, 2000.

Lomong, Lopez. *Running for My Life: One Lost Boy's Journey from the Killing Fields of Sudan to the Olympic Games*. Nashville, TN: Thomas Nelson, 2012.

Lowry, Lois. *Looking Back: A Book of Memories*. New York: Houghton Mifflin, 1998.

Luttrell, Marcus. *Lone Survivor: The Eye Witness Account of Operation Red Wing and the Lost Heroes of SEAL Team 10*. New York: Back Bay Books, 2007.

Ma, Yan and Haski, Pierre. *The Diary of Ma Yan: The Struggles and Hopes of a Chinese Schoolgirl*. New York: HarperCollins, 2009.

Maathai, Wangari. *Unbowed: A Memoir*. New York: Anchor Books, 2007.

Mahlendorf. Ursula. *The Shame of Survival: Working Through a Nazi Childhood*. University Park, PA: The Pennsylvania State University Press, 2009.

Mathabane, Mark. *Kaffir Boy: The True Story of a Black Youth's Coming of Age in Apartheid*. New York: Plume, 1987.

Maynard, Kyle. *No Excuses: The True Story of a Congenital Amputee Who Became a Champion in Wrestling and in Life*. Washington, DC: Regnery Publishing, 2005.

McCourt, Frank. *Angela's Ashes: A Memoir*. New York: Simon & Schuster, 2000.

McCourt, Frank. *'Tis: A Memoir*. New York: Simon & Schuster, 2000.

McDonough, Mary. *Lessons from the Mountain: What I Learned from Erin Walton*. New York: Kensington Publishing Corp., 2011.

McGough, Matthew. *Bat Boy: Coming of Age with the New York Yankees*. New York: Anchor Books, 2007.

Menzie, Morgan. *Diary of an Anorexic Girl* [fictionalized memoir]. Nashville, TN: Thomas Nelson, 2003.

Miskimen, Mel C. *Cop's Kid: A Milwaukee Memoir*. Madison, WI: University of Wisconsin Press, 2003.

Moore, Wes. *The Other Wes Moore: One Name, Two Fates*. New York: Spiegel & Grau, 2011.

Mortenson, Greg and Relin, David Oliver. *Three Cups of Tea*. New York: Puffin Books, 2009.

Myers, Walter Dean. *Bad Boy, A Memoir*. New York: Amistad, 2002.

Naylor, Phyllis Reynolds. *How I Came to Be a Writer*. New York: Atheneum Books for Young Readers, 2001.

Nelson, George. *City Kid: A Writer's Memoir of Ghetto Life and Post-Soul Success*. New York: Plume, 2010.

Nhuong, Huynh Quang. *Water Buffalo Days: Growing Up in Vietnam*. New York: HarperCollins Publishers, 1999.

Nixon, Joan Lowery. *The Making of a Writer*. New York: Delacorte Books for Young Readers, 2002.

Obama, Barack. *Dreams From My Father: A Story of Race and Inheritance*. New York: Three Rivers Press, 2004.

Opdyke, Irene Gut. *In My Hands: Memories of a Holocaust Rescuer*. New York: Alfred A. Knopf, 1999.

Paulsen, Gary. *Caught By the Sea: My Life on Boats*. New York: Dell Laurel-Leaf, 2001.

Paulsen, Gary. *Father Water, Mother Woods*. New York: Dell Laurel-Leaf, 2001.

Paulsen, Gary. *Guts*. New York: Dell Laurel-Leaf, 2001.

Paulsen, Gary. *My Life in Dog Years*. New York: Yearling, 1999.

Paulsen, Gary. *Winterdance: The Fine Madness of Running the Iditarod*. New York: Mariner Books, 1995.

Peet, Bill. *Bill Peet: An Autobiography*. New York: HMH Books for Young Readers, 1994.

Pelzer, Dave. *A Child Called It: A Child's Courage to Survive*. Deerfield Beach, FL: Health Communications, 1995.

Pelzer, Dave. *The Lost Boy: A Foster Child's Search for the Love of a Family*. Deerfield Beach, FL: Health Communications, 2010.

Pelzer, Dave. *A Man Named Dave*. New York: Plume, 2000.

Pelzer, Dave. *The Privilege of Youth*. New York: Plume, 2004.

Perham, Mike. *Sailing the Dream: The Amazing True Story of the Teen Who Sailed Solo Around the World*. Lebanon, NH: University Press of New England, 2011.

Ragusa, Kym. *The Skin Between Us: A Memoir of Race, Beauty, and Belonging*. New York: W.W. Norton & Company, 2006.

Rhoads-Courter, Ashley. *Three Little Words: a Memoir*. New York: Atheneum Books for Young Readers, 2009.

Richardson, Kevin. *Part of the Pride: My Life Among the Big Cats of Africa*. New York: St. Martin's Press, 2009.

Robison, John Elder. *Look Me in the Eye: My Life with Asperger's*. New York: Three Rivers Press, 2008.

Rodriguez, Gaby. *The Pregnancy Project: A Memoir*. New York: Simon & Schuster Books for Young Readers, 2013.

Rodriguez, Luis J. *Always Running, La Vida Loca: Gang Days in L. A.* New York: Simon & Schuster, 2005.

Rouse, Wade. *America's Boy: A Memoir*. New York: Plume, 2007.

Runyon, Brent. *The Burn Journals*. New York: Vintage Books, 2004.

Rylant, Cynthia. *But I'll Be Back Again*. New York: HarperCollins, 1993.

Salzman, Mark. *Lost in Place: Growing up Absurd in Suburbia*. New York: Vintage Books, 1996.

Santiago, Esmeralda. *When I Was Puerto Rican*. New York: Vintage Books, 1998.

Satrapi, Marjane. *The Complete Persepolis*. New York: Pantheon Books, 2007.

Say, Allen. *Drawing From Memory*. New York: Scholastic, 2011.

Scieszka, Jon. *Knucklehead: Tall Tales and Almost True Stories of Growing Up Scieszka*. New York: Viking Juvenile, 2008.

Sleator, William. *Oddballs*. New York: Puffin Books, 1993.

Small, David. *Stitches: A Memoir*. New York: W. W. Norton & Company, 2009.

Sones, Sonya. *Stop Pretending: What Happened When My Big Sister Went Crazy*. New York: HarperTempest, 2006.

Soto, Gary. *A Summer Life*. New York: Laurel-Leaf Books, 1991.

Sparks, Beatrice, Ed. *Annie's Baby: The Diary of Anonymous, Pregnant Teenager*. New York: Avon Books, 2005.

Spears, Lynne. *Through the Storm: A Real Story of Fame and Family in a Tabloid World*. Nashville: Thomas Nelson, 2008.

Spinelli, Jerry. *Knots in my Yo-yo String: The Autobiography of a Kid*. New York: Alfred A. Knopf, 1998.

Summer, Lauralee. *Learning Joy From Dogs Without Collars, a Memoir*. New York: Simon & Schuster, 2004.

*Tan, Amy. *The Joy Luck Club*. New York: Vintage, 1991.

Taylor, Blake E. S. *ADHD & Me: What I Learned from Lighting Fires at The Dinner Table*. Oakland, CA: New Harbinger Publications, 2007.

Telgemeier, Rania. *Smile*. New York: Graphix, 2010.

Thoms, Annie, Ed. *With Their Eyes*. New York: HarperTempest, 2002.

Trope, Zoe. *Please Don't Kill the Freshman: A Memoir*. New York: HarperCollins, 2004.

Uchida, Yoshiko. *The Invisible Thread*. New York: HarperTrophy, 1995.

von Trapp, Maria Augusta. *The Story of the Trapp Family Singers*. New York, William Morrow Paperbacks, 2001.

Walls, Jeannette. *The Glass Castle*. New York: Scribner, 2006.

Weisel, Elie. *All Rivers Run to the Sea: Memoirs*. New York: Shocken Books, 1995.

Weisel, Elie. *Night*. New York: Hill and Wang, 2006.

Wheatley, Sharon. *'Till the Fat Girl Sings: From an Overweight Nobody to a Broadway Somebody—a Memoir*. Avon, MA: Adams Media, 2006.

White, Ryan. *Ryan White: My Own Story*. New York: Signet, 1992.

Wiesenthal, Simon. *The Sunflower: On the Possibilities and Limits of Forgiveness*. New York: Shocken Books, 1997.

Wolfe, Swain. *The Boy Who Invented Skiing: A Memoir*. New York: St. Martin's Press, 2006.

Wolff, Tobias. *This Boy's Life: A Memoir*. New York: Grove Press, 1989.

Wright, Richard. *Black Boy (American Hunger): A Record of Childhood and Youth*. New York: Perennial Classics, 1998.

Yen Mah, Adeline. *Chinese Cinderella: The True Story of an Unwanted Daughter*. New York: Dell Laurel-Leaf, 1999.

Yep, Lawrence. *The Lost Garden*. New York: HarperCollins, 1996.

Yoran, Shalom. *The Defiant: A True Story of Escape, Survival & Resistance*. Garden City Park, NY: Square One Publishers, 2003.

Yousafzai, Malala and Lamb, Christina. *I Am Malala: The Girl Who Stood Up for Education and Was Shot by the Talaban*. New York: Little, Brown and Company, 2013.

Zenatti, Valerie. *When I Was a Soldier*. New York: Bloomsbury U.S.A. Children's Books, 2007.

Zindel, Paul. *The Pigman & Me*. New York: Bantam Books, 1993.

* Memoirs listed in Common Core State Standards Appendix C as an exemplar nonfiction text

APPENDIX C
Resources for Writers

Gertler, Nat and Steve Lieber. *The Complete Idiot's Guide to Creating a Graphic Novel.* New York: Alpha Books, 2004.

Grambs, David. *The Describer's Dictionary: A Treasury of Terms & Literary Quotations.* New York: W. W. Norton & Company, 1995.

Hall, Robin. *The Cartoonist's Workbook.* New York: Main Street, 2004.

Harley, Avis. *Fly with Poetry: An ABC of Poetry.* Honesdale, PA: Wordsong, 2000.

Hoff, Syd. *The Young Cartoonist: The ABC's of Cartooning.* New York: Stravon Educational Press, 1990.

Janeczko, Paul B., Ed. *A Kick in the Head: An Everyday Guide to Poetic Forms.* Somerville, MA: Candlewick Press, 2009.

Mazer, Anne and Ellen Potter. *Spilling Ink: A Young Writer's Handbook.* New York: Roaring Brook Press, 2010.

Strunk, William, Jr. and E. B. White. *The Elements of Style, Pearson New International Edition.* Essex: Pearson Education Limited, 2014.

Young, Judy. *R Is for Rhyme: A Poetry Alphabet.* Ann Arbor, MI: Sleeping Bear Press, 2010.

Young, Sue. *Scholastic Rhyming Dictionary.* New York: Scholastic, Inc., 1997.

Zinsser, William, Ed. *Inventing the Truth: The Art and Craft of Memoir.* New York: Houghton Mifflin Company, 1998.

Zinsser, William. *On Writing Well, 30th Anniversary Edition: The Classic Guide to Writing Nonfiction.* New York: HarperPerennial, 2006.

RESOURCES FOR TEACHING WRITERS

Atwell, Nancie. *Lessons That Change Writers.* Portsmouth, NH: Heinemann, 2007.

Culham, Ruth. *Traits of Writing: The Complete Guide for Middle School.* New York: Scholastic Teaching Resources, 2010.

Hicks, Troy. *Crafting Digital Writing: Composing Texts across Media and Genres.* Portsmouth, NH: Heinemann, 2013.

Kajder, Sara. *Adolescents and Digital Literacies: Learning Alongside Our Students.* Urbana, IL: NCTE, 2010.

Kirby, Dan, Dawn Latta Kirby, and Tom Liner. *Inside Out: Strategies for Teaching Writing, Third Edition.* Portsmouth, NH: Heinemann, 2004.

Lane, Barry. *After "The End": Teaching and Learning Creative Revision.* Portsmouth, NH: Heinemann, 1992.

——. *The Reviser's Toolbox.* Shoreham, VT: Discover Writing Press, 1999.

Miller, Lisa C. *Make Me a Story: Teaching Writing Through Digital Storytelling.* Portland, ME: Stenhouse Publishers, 2010.

Ray, Katie Wood. *Wondrous Words: Writers and Writing in the Elementary Classroom,* Urbana, Illinois: National Council of Teachers of English, 1999.

Roessing, Lesley. *The Write to Read: Response Journals That Increase Comprehension.* Thousand Oaks, CA: Corwin Press, 2009.

Spandel, Vicki. *Creating Writers Through 6-Trait Writing Assessment and Instruction* (5th Edition). New York: Pearson, 2008.

APPENDIX D

Reproducible Forms for Readers and Writers

REPRODUCIBLE 1: SENSORY MEMORY TRIGGERS

Sense Memory Triggers

Sense	Trigger	Memory
Smell		
Taste		
Sound		
Touch		
Sight		

REPRODUCIBLE 2: MEMORIES CHART

Memories

PEOPLE				
Relatives	Friends	Neighbors	Teachers & Classmates	Other

PLACES				
Homes/Rooms	Vacations	Schools	Special Places	Other

POSSESSIONS				
Toys	Games	Crafts	Clothing & Jewelry	Other

RECREATION				
Outside Game	Sports	Activities	Hobbies	Lessons

REPRODUCIBLE 3: MEMORIES CHART

Memories

ANIMALS				
Pets	Stuffed/Toy	Stories	Wild	

SENSE MEMORIES (IMAGERY)				
Tastes	Smells	Tactile	Sounds	Visual

IMPORTANT MOMENTS				
Decisions	Beliefs	Medical	School	Family

OTHER MEMORIES				
Family Sayings	Religion	Meals/Foods	————	————

REPRODUCIBLE 4: HEART MAP

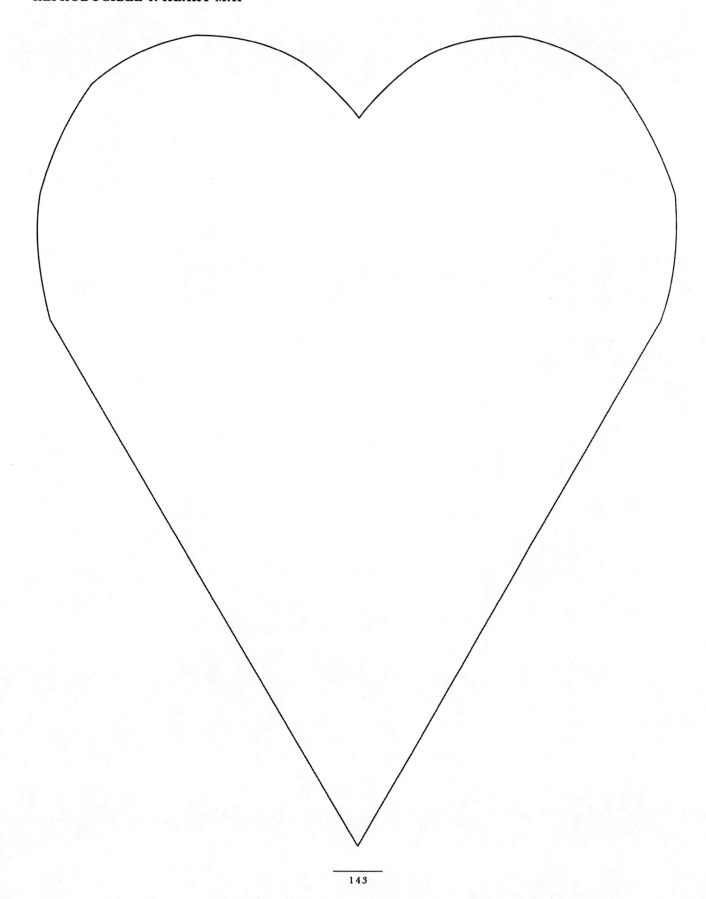

REPRODUCIBLE 5: SMALL-MOMENT MEMORIES CHART

Small-Moment Memories

PERSON SMALL MOMENT	PERSON SMALL MOMENT	PERSON SMALL MOMENT	PET SMALL MOMENT
PLACE SMALL MOMENT	PLACE SMALL MOMENT	ACTIVITY SMALL MOMENT	ACTIVITY SMALL MOMENT
OBJECT SMALL MOMENT	OBJECT SMALL MOMENT	OBJECT SMALL MOMENT	TOY/GAME SMALL MOMENT
IMPORTANT EVENT SMALL MOMENT	IMPORTANT EVENT SMALL MOMENT	DECISION SMALL MOMENT	_____ SMALL MOMENT

REPRODUCIBLE 6: SMALL-MOMENT MEMORIES CHART

Small-Moment Memories (page 2)

AGES/TIME				
AGE/TIME SMALL MOMENT	AGE/TIME SMALL MOMENT	AGE/TIME SMALL MOMENT	AGE/TIME SMALL MOMENT	AGE/TIME SMALL MOMENT
PHOTOGRAPH/ARTIFACT				
PHOTOGRAPH SMALL MOMENT	PHOTOGRAPH SMALL MOMENT	PHOTOGRAPH SMALL MOMENT	PHOTOGRAPH SMALL MOMENT	PHOTOGRAPH SMALL MOMENT
CRISES				
CRISIS SMALL MOMENT	CRISIS SMALL MOMENT	CRISIS SMALL MOMENT	CRISIS SMALL MOMENT	CRISIS SMALL MOMENT
Other Memories				

REPRODUCIBLE 7: MEMOIR DOUBLE-ENTRY RESPONSE JOURNAL

Memoir Double-Entry Response Journal

Quote/Information from Book	My Thoughts on **What** the Author Writes

REPRODUCIBLE 8: MEMOIR DOUBLE-ENTRY RESPONSE JOURNAL

Memoir Double-Entry Response Journal

Quote/Information from Book	My Thoughts on **How** the Author Writes

REPRODUCIBLE 9: MEMOIR TRIPLE-COLUMN RESPONSE JOURNAL

Memoir Triple-Column Response Journal

What the Author Wrote (Quote/Information)	My Thoughts	What I Might Try in My Writing

REPRODUCIBLE 10: MEMORY TIME-GRAPH

In each box, chronologically draw pictures of memories of certain ages.

	Year I Was Born	Year I Was 1	Year I Was 2	Year I Was 3	Year I Was 4	Year I Was 5	Year I Was 6	Year I Was 7
Birthday								
3 months								
6 months								
9 months								

REPRODUCIBLE 11: AGE PROS & CONS CHART

Pros & Cons Chart of Turning _____

PROS	CONS

REPRODUCIBLE 12: CRISIS RESPONSE JOURNAL

Crisis Response Journal

A Crisis	What Led to the Crisis	The Outcome or How the Crisis Affected the Author	Affective Words, Terms, or Phrases the Author Used

WORKS CITED

Abeel, Samantha. *My Thirteenth Winter: A Memoir.* New York: Scholastic, 2005.

Albers, Donald J. and Alexanderson, Gerald L., eds. *Fascinating Mathematical People: Interviews and Memoirs.* Princeton, NJ: Princeton University Press, 2011.

Anthony, Lawrence. *The Elephant Whisperer: My Life with the Herd in the African Wild.* New York: St. Martin's Griffin, 2012.

Aronson, Roy. *Tales of an African Vet.* Guilford, CT: Lyons Press, 2011.

Atwell, Nancie. *In the Middle: New Understandings about Writing, Reading, and Learning.* Portsmouth, NH: Heinemann, 1998. Print.

———. *Lessons That Change Writers.* Portsmouth, NH: Heinemann, 2002. Print.

Audet, Cynthia. "Scar." *The Sun.* January 2003. Print.

Bouchard, David. *If you're not from the prairie...* New York: Aladdin Paperbacks, 1998. Print.

Bradby, Marie. *Momma, Where Are You From?* New York: Orchard, 2000. Print.

Chin, Beverly Ann. "Teaching Meaningful Revision: Developing and Deepening Students' Writing." *Professional Development Series, Volume 15.* http://www.sadlieroxford.com/prof_development/peerrewchin.cfm?page=0, accessed 2/11/14.

Cisneros, Sandra. "Eleven." *Woman Hollering Creek.* New York: Vintage, 1992. Print.

Collins, Billy. "The Lanyard." *The Trouble with Poetry: And Other Poems.* New York: Random House, 2005. Print.

———. "On Turning Ten." *Art of Drowning.* Pittsburgh: University of Pittsburgh Press, 1995. Print.

Cosby, Bill. *The Best of Bill Cosby.* New York: Warner Bros. Records Inc., 2005. CD.

———. *Wonderfulness.* New York: Warner Bros. Records Inc., 1966. CD.

Dahl, Roald. *Boy.* New York: Farrar, Straus And Giroux, 1986. Print.

Degre, Tippi. *Tippi: My Book of Africa.* Cape Town, South Africa: Random House Struik, 2012.

Donne, John. "Meditation XVII." *The Works of John Donne, Vol III.* Alford, Henry, ed. London: John W. Parker, 1839. 574-5. Print.

Ehrlich, Amy, ed. *When I was Your Age: Original Stories About Growing Up, Volume One.* Cambridge, MA: Candlewick Press, 1996. Print.

———. *When I Was Your Age: Original Stories About Growing Up, Volume Two.* Cambridge, MA: Candlewick Press, 2002.

Firestein, Stuart. Interview by Andrew Dermont. "Unlocking the Mysterious Connection Between Taste, Smell, and Memory." *bigthink.com/videos/ unlocking-the-mysterious-connection-between-taste-smell-and-memory.* big think. Recorded September 22, 2010. Web. 21 Dec 2013.

Fox, Mem. *Wilfrid Gordon McDonald Partridge.* New York: Puffin Books, 1992. Print.

Georges, Christopher J. and Georges, Gigi E., with members of the staff of the *Harvard Independent,* eds. *100 Successful College Application Essays.* New York: Plume, 1988. Print.

Giovanni, Nikki. *Knoxville, Tennessee.* Scholastic, 1994. Print.

Goldstein, Kenneth Roy. "Notes from the Past—A Memoir." *Aaron's Intifada And Other Short Stories.* Lincoln, NE: iUniverse, 2002. Print.

Gonick, Larry. *The Cartoon History of the United States.* New York: Collins Reference, 1991. Print.

Goyer, Amy. "More Grandparents Raising Grandkids." *AARP.org.* 12-20-2010. Web. 31 Dec. 2013. www.aarp.org/relationships/grandparenting/info-12-2010/more_grandparents_raising_grandchildren.html

Graham, Steve, and Michael Hebert. *Writing to Read: Evidence for How Writing Can Improve. Carnegie Corporation Time to Act Report*. Washington, DC: Alliance for Excellent Education, 2010. Print.

Gustafson, Karl. *The Crossing of Heaven: Memoirs of a Mathematician*. Heidelberg, Germany: Springer, 2012.

Hadfield, Chris. *An Astronaut's Guide to Life on Earth: What Going to Space Taught Me About Ingenuity, Determination, and Being Prepared for Anything.* . New York: Little, Brown and Company, 2013.

Heard, Georgia. *Awakening the Heart: Exploring Poetry in Elementary and Middle School*. Portsmouth, NH: Heinemann, 1998. Print.

Herriot, James. *All Creatures Great and Small*. New York: Bantam Books, 1989.

Hickam, Homer H., Jr. *Rocket Boys*. New York: Dell Publishing, 1998.

Hirsch, Edward. "Proustian." *The Night Parade: Poems*. New York: Knopf, 2003. Print.

Holahan, David. "When Lobsters Run Free." *Philadelphia Inquirer*, April 23, 2006. Print.

Jacobson, Sid and Colón, Ernie. *Anne Frank: The Anne Frank House Authorized Graphic Biography*. New York: Hill and Wang, 2010. Print.

Janecko, Paul B. "Bingo." *The Place My Words Are Looking For: What Poets Say About and Through Their Work*. Janecko, Paul B., Ed. New York: Bradbury, 1990. Print.

Kenyon, Jane. "Trouble with Math in a One-room Country School." *Collected Poems*. Minneapolis, MN: Graywolf Press, 2005. Print.

Kim, Derek Kirk. "Hurdles." *Same Difference and Other Stories*. Marietta, GA: Top Shelf Productions, 2004. Print.

Kohn, Alfie. "How to Create Nonreaders: Reflections on Motivation, Learning, and Sharing Power. *English Journal*. Sept. 2010: 16-22. Print.

Leigh, Richard C and Martine, Layng, Jr. "The Greatest Man I Never Knew." McEntire, Reba. *For My Broken Heart*. MCA Records, 1991. [CD]

L'Engle, Madelaine and Larson, Hope. *A Wrinkle in Time: The Graphic Novel*. Farrar, Straus and Giroux, 2012. Print.

Lyon, George Ella. "Where I'm From." *Where I'm From, Where Poems Come From*. Spring, TX: Absey & Company, Inc., 1999. Print.

Mah, Adeline Yen. *Chinese Cinderella: The True Story of an Unwanted Daughter*. New York: Dell Laurel-Leaf, 1999. Print.

Meyer, Stephanie and Young, Kim. *Twilight, the Graphic Novel, Vol 1*. New York: Yen Press, 2012. Print.

Micklos, John. *Grandparent Poems*. Honesdale, PA: Wordsong, 2004. Print.

Mori, Kyoto. "Learning to Swim." *When I was Your Age: Original Stories About Growing Up, Volume Two*. Ed. Amy Ehrlich. Cambridge, MA: Candlewick Press, 2002. Print.

National Governors Association Center for Best Practices & Council of Chief State School Officers. (2010). *Common Core State Standards for English language arts and literacy in history/social studies, science, and technical subjects*. Washington, DC: Authors.

Neri, G. *Yummy: The Last Days of a Southside Shorty*. New York: Lee & Low Books, 2010. Print.

Nerudo, Pablo. "Ode to the Tomato." *Neruda, Selected Poems*. New York: Houghton Mifflin, 1990. Print.

Neufield, Josh. *A.D. New Orleans After the Deluge*. New York: Pantheon, 2010. Print.

Osborne, Mary Pope. "All Ball." *When I was Your Age: Original Stories About Growing Up, Volume One*. Ed. Amy Ehrlich. Cambridge, MA: Candlewick Press, 1996. Print.

Parton, Dolly. "Coat of Many Colors." *Coat of Many Colors*. RCA Records. 1971. Vinyl.

——. *Coat of Many Colors*. New York: HarperCollins, 1996. Print.

Paulsen, Gary. "Introduction." *Shelf Talk: Stories by the Book*. Simon & Schuster for Young Readers, 2003. Print.

Polacco, Patricia. *Betty Doll*. New York: Philomel, 2001. Print.

——. *The Keeping Quilt*. New York: Simon & Schuster for Young Readers, 1988. Print.

——. *Meteor*. New York: Puffin, 1996. Print.

——. *My Ol' Man*. New York: Puffin, 1999. Print.

——. *My Rotten Redheaded Older Brother*. New York: Aladdin, 1994. Print.

——. *Some Birthday*. New York: Simon & Schuster, 1993. Print.

——. *Thunder Cake*. New York: Puffin, 1997. Print.

Proust, Marcel. *Remembrance of Things Past: Volume 1*. New York: Vintage, 1982.

Richardson, Kevin. *Part of the Pride: My Life Among the Big Cats of Africa*. New York: St. Martin's Press, 2009.

Rockwell, Norman. *The Discovery*. 1956. Oil on canvas. Norman Rockwell Museum, Stockbridge, MA.

Rodriguez, Luis J. *Always Running: La Vida Loca, Gang Days in L.A.* Willimantic, CT: Curbstone, 1993. Print.

——. "Race Politics." *Cool Salsa: Bilingual Poems on Growing Up Latino in the United States*. Ed. Lori M. Carlson. New York: Henry Holt and Company, Inc., 1994. Print.

Roessing, Lesley. "Back in the Hood." *No More "Us" and "Them": Classroom Lessons & Activities to Promote Peer Respect.* Lanham, MD: Rowman & Littlefield, 2012. Print.

——. "Teenagers." *No More "Us" and "Them": Classroom Lessons & Activities to Promote Peer Respect.* Lanham, MD: Rowman & Littlefield, 2012. Print.

——. *The Write to Read: Response Journals That Increase Comprehension.* Thousand Oaks, CA: Corwin Press, 2009. Print.

——. "Writing to Learn: Using Poetry in Two Voices." *Middle Ground,* 16(3), 2013. Print.

Russo, Marisabina. *Always Remember Me: How One Family Survived World War II.* Atheneum for Young Readers, 2005. Print.

Rylant, Cynthia. *Missing May.* New York: Scholastic, 2004.

——. *The Relatives Came.* New York: Aladdin, 1985. Print.

——. *Waiting to Waltz: A Childhood.* New York: Atheneum/Richard Jackson Books, 2001. Print.

——. *When I Was Young in the Mountains.* New York: Penguin Group, 1993. Print.

Santiago, Esmeralda. *When I was Puerto Rican.* New York: Vintage Books, 1998.

Satrapi, Marjane. *Persepolis: The Story of a Childhood.* New York: Pantheon Books, 2004. Print.

Schotter, Roni. *Nothing Ever Happens on 90th Street.* New York: Scholastic, 1999. Print.

Scottoline, Lisa. *Mistaken Identity.* New York: HarperTorch, 2002. Print.

Sones, Sonya. *Stop Pretending: What Happened When My Big Sister Went Crazy.* New York: HarperTempest, 1999. Print.

Soto, Gary. *Neighborhood Odes.* New York: Harcourt, Inc., 2005. Print.

Spiegelman, Art. "Eye Ball." *Breakdowns: Portrait of the Artist as a Young %@&*!* New York: Pantheon, 2008. Print.

——. *Maus I: A Survivor's Tale—My Father Bleeds History.* New York: Pantheon Books, 1986. Print.

——. *Maus II: A Survivor's Tale—And Here My Troubles Began.* New York: Pantheon Books, 1991. Print.

Stafford, William. "Things I Learned Last Week." *Sound of the Ax: Aphorism and Poems by William Stafford.* Eds. Vincent Wixon and Paul Merchant. Pittsburgh: University of Pittsburgh Press, 2014.

——. "What's In My Journal?" *Crossing Unmarked Snow: Further Views on the Writer's Vocation.* Ann Arbor: University of Michigan, 1998. Print.

Vinz, Mark. "What I Remember About Sixth Grade." *Late Night Calls.* Moorhead, MN: New Rivers Press, 1992. Print.

Viorst, Judith. "Since Hannah Moved Away." *If I Were in Charge of the World and Other Worries.* New York: Macmillan, 1981. Print.

Webb, Charles. "The Death of Santa Claus." *Reading the Water.* Boston: Northeastern University Press, 2001. Print.

Woodson, Jacqueline. *Sweet, Sweet Memory.* New York: Jump at the Sun/Hyperion for Children, 2000. Print.

Yang, Gene Luen. *American Born Chinese.* New York: Square Fish, 2008. Print.

Yolen, Jane. "The Long Closet." *When I Was Your Age: Volume Two.* Ed. Amy Ehrlich. Cambridge, MA: Candlewick Press, 2002. Print.

Young, Judy. *R is for Rhyme: A Poetry Alphabet.* Ann Arbor, MI: Sleeping Bear Press, 2010. Print.

Zinnser, William. *On Writing Well, 30th Anniversary Edition: The Classic Guide to Writing Nonfiction.* New York: Harper Perennial, 2006.

CPSIA information can be obtained at www.ICGtesting.com
Printed in the USA
BVOW06s1212230714

360167BV00006B/13/P